MARSHALL MINI
DINOSAURS

Sue Nicholson

MARSHALL PUBLISHING • LONDON

Contents

Age of the dinosaurs

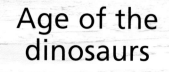

A pack of *Coelophysis* hunt by a drying lake in North America during the Triassic Period, 220 million years ago.

When the dinosaurs lived

Dinosaurs ruled the Earth for an amazing 165 million years. The first dinosaurs appeared about 230 million years ago. They became extinct, or died out, 65 million years ago.

PALAEOZOIC
540 to 250

Periods of time

Scientists divide the Earth's history into eras, and eras are divided into periods. The Mesozoic Era, from 250 to 65 million years ago, was the Age of Dinosaurs. It is divided into three periods – the Triassic, Jurassic and Cretaceous periods.

The first dinosaurs evolved about 230 million years ago.

MESOZOIC ERA
250 to 65 MYA

Anchisaurus – *an early plant-eating dinosaur*

CENOZOIC ERA
65 MYA to present day

8

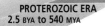

PROTEROZOIC ERA
2.5 BYA to 540 MYA

Dicksonia

The simplest forms of life first appeared in the Earth's oceans about 3.5 billion years ago.

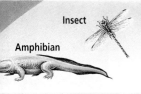

Insect

Amphibian

Trilobite

Creatures called trilobites first lived 530 million years ago. Insects and amphibians evolved 400 million years ago.

TRIASSIC PERIOD

Procompsognathus

Cynognathus
(mammal-like reptile)

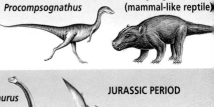

Ichthyosaur

Brachiosaurus

JURASSIC PERIOD

Coelurus

Stegosaurus

Pterosaur

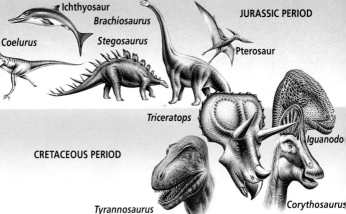

Triceratops

Iguanodo

CRETACEOUS PERIOD

Tyrannosaurus

Corythosaurus

BYA = billion years ago
MYA = million years ago

The Triassic Period

The Triassic Period lasted 45 million years, from 250 to 205 million years ago. It is named after the Latin word *trias* (three) because European rocks of the time can be divided into three ages.

The Triassic landscape

The Earth was much drier during the Triassic Period than it is today. There were hot, dry deserts in inland areas, far from the sea. Most plants grew around lakes or by pools of water that formed after rain but later dried up. The plants provided food for plant-eating animals which, in turn, provided food for the meat eaters.

Plant life

Large plants included yews and ginkgoes, or maidenhair trees. Ferns, tree ferns and horsetails grew in damper areas. There were no flowering plants or grasses. These evolved much later, during the Cretaceous Period.

Ginkgo leaf

10

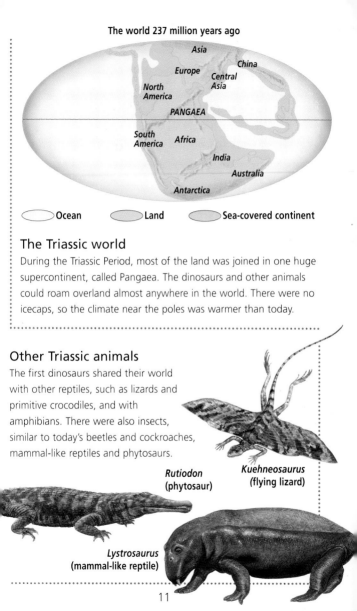

The world 237 million years ago

Asia

China

Europe

Central Asia

North America

PANGAEA

South America

Africa

India

Australia

Antarctica

Ocean   Land   Sea-covered continent

The Triassic world

During the Triassic Period, most of the land was joined in one huge supercontinent, called Pangaea. The dinosaurs and other animals could roam overland almost anywhere in the world. There were no icecaps, so the climate near the poles was warmer than today.

Other Triassic animals

The first dinosaurs shared their world with other reptiles, such as lizards and primitive crocodiles, and with amphibians. There were also insects, similar to today's beetles and cockroaches, mammal-like reptiles and phytosaurs.

Rutiodon (phytosaur)

Kuehneosaurus (flying lizard)

Lystrosaurus (mammal-like reptile)

11

The Jurassic Period

The Jurassic Period lasted 65 million years, from 205 to 140 million years ago. It is named after the limestone that formed at this time in the sea and later became part of the European Jura Mountains.

The Jurassic landscape

The dry deserts of the Triassic Period mostly disappeared during the early Jurassic Period. The climate was not as hot, but it was still warmer than it is today. There was also plenty of rain. Plants flourished in the warm, wet climate. Many were large and lush, like the plants of today's tropical rainforests. Forest trees included tree ferns, giant cone-bearing conifer trees similar to today's pines and larches, ginkgoes and cycads.

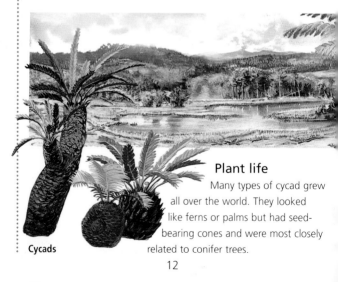

Plant life

Many types of cycad grew all over the world. They looked like ferns or palms but had seed-bearing cones and were most closely related to conifer trees.

Cycads

The world 160 million years ago

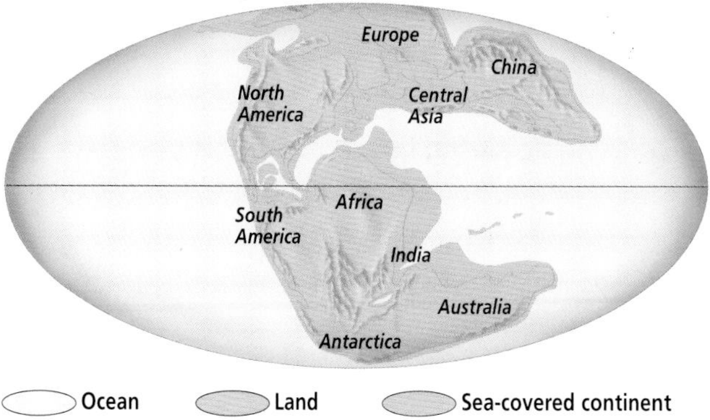

Ocean   Land   Sea-covered continent

The Jurassic world

By the end of the Jurassic Period, Pangaea had started to break
up into separate continents. What is now North America had
drifted away from South America and the two continents
were separated by sea.

Other Jurassic animals

During the Jurassic Period, the world's
oceans were home to a huge range of
animals, including ichthyosaurs and
plesiosaurs. Mammal-like reptiles and
early crocodiles lived on land, while
flying reptiles flew through the sky.

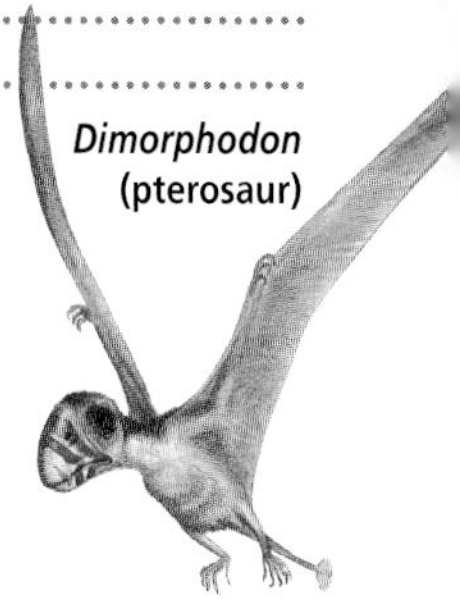

Dimorphodon
(pterosaur)

Ophthalmosaurus
(marine reptile)

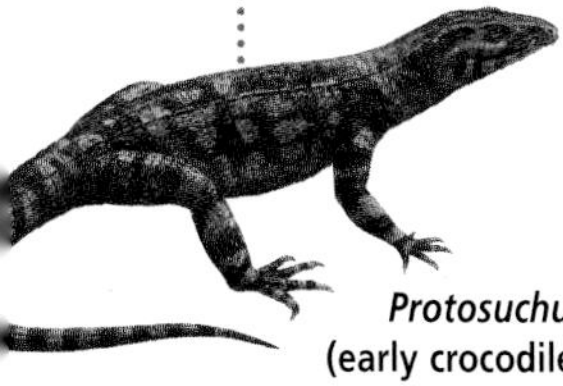

Protosuchus
(early crocodile)

Oligokyphus
(mammal-like
reptile)

The Cretaceous Period

The Cretaceous Period lasted 75 million years, from 140 to 65 million years ago. Its name comes from a Latin word meaning "of chalk" and refers to chalk deposits laid down in shallow seas at the time.

Cretaceous landscape

Flowering plants slowly evolved during the Cretaceous Period. Eventually, they dominated the landscape instead of the ferns, horsetails and cycads common during Jurassic times.

Plant life

By the end of the Cretaceous Period, a wide variety of plants had evolved. These included hickory trees, oaks and magnolias as well as smaller flowering plants.

14

The world 80 million years ago

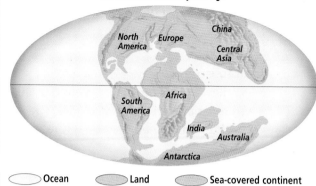

◯ Ocean ◯ Land ◯ Sea-covered continent

The Cretaceous world

During the Cretaceous Period, the landmasses drifted still farther apart. Towards the end of the period, shallow seas covered much of North America and Europe, for a time dividing each continent.

Other Cretaceous animals

New types of animal evolved during the Cretaceous Period, including new kinds of dinosaur. Pterosaurs, which had flourished during the Jurassic Period, still ruled the skies. There were also many kinds of reptile, including crocodiles, snakes, turtles and lizards.

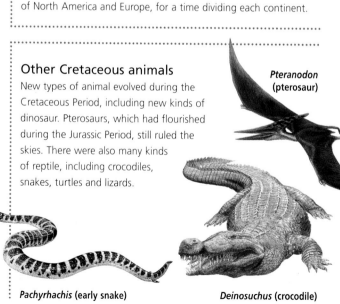

Pteranodon (pterosaur)

Pachyrhachis (early snake)

Deinosuchus (crocodile)

What is a dinosaur?

**The word dinosaur means "terrible lizard".
Like modern lizards, the dinosaurs were reptiles.
They laid eggs, as today's reptiles do, and they
had scaly skin.**

Reptile egg   **Amphibian egg**

Reptile eggs

Amphibian eggs, such as frog spawn,
are coated in jelly and are laid in water.
Reptile eggs are tougher, with leathery
or hard shells. The shells help to protect
the baby reptile as it grows. When it
hatches, a reptile is like a miniature
adult. Most reptiles are able to
look after themselves as soon
as they are born.

New way of moving

Dinosaurs evolved a better way of moving than
other reptiles. Early reptiles moved in the same way
as modern lizards, by twisting their bodies from
side to side with each step. Dinosaurs held their
legs straight underneath their bodies. This
meant their legs could carry more
weight and many dinosaurs
became bigger and heavier.

Lizard   **Dinosaur**

16

Scaly skin

Although we know that dinosaurs
had scaly skin, we do not know what
colour it was. Just as modern reptiles,
some may have been brightly coloured
to warn off meat eaters, while others
may have been dull colours, for
camouflage.

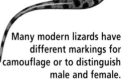

**Many modern lizards have
different markings for
camouflage or to distinguish
male and female.**

Dinosaur groups

Dinosaurs can be divided into two main orders, or groups,
depending on the structure of their hip bones. In saurischian,
or lizard-hipped, dinosaurs, the pubis bone points away from
the ischium bone. This group includes some plant eaters and
all the meat-eating dinosaurs. In ornithischian, or bird-hipped,
dinosaurs, the pubis bone runs below
the ischium bone. This group
were all plant eaters.

Pubis

Ischium

**Skeleton of
Iguanodon, an
ornithischian
dinosaur**

Ischium

Pubis

**Skeleton of
Ornitholestes, a
saurischian
dinosaur**

17

Dinosaur groups

This chart shows how the two main dinosaur orders – saurischia (saurischian dinosaurs) and ornithischia (ornithischian dinosaurs) – can be divided into smaller groups and families.

SAURISCHIA

THEROPODA

DINOSAURIA

SAUROPODOMORPHA

ORNITHISCHIA

GENASAURIA

Fact boxes in the guide to dinosaurs section (pages 66–109) have been colour coded to match this chart.

THYREOPHORA

CERAPODA

Dinosaur families

The two main orders of dinosaurs are divided into suborders. For example, the saurischian dinosaurs are divided into theropods (theropoda) and sauropods (sauropodomorpha). Suborders are divided still further into infraorders, divisions and families. Some families contain only one known species of dinosaur. In this case, the genus name (for example, *Compsognathus*) is given instead of the family name (the name ending in -idae). Other families contain several species of dinosaur. For example, the family Hadrosauridae (the hadrosaurs) contains about 10 genera, or types, of dinosaur, including *Pachycephalosaurus*, *Lambeosaurus* and *Edmontosaurus*.

18

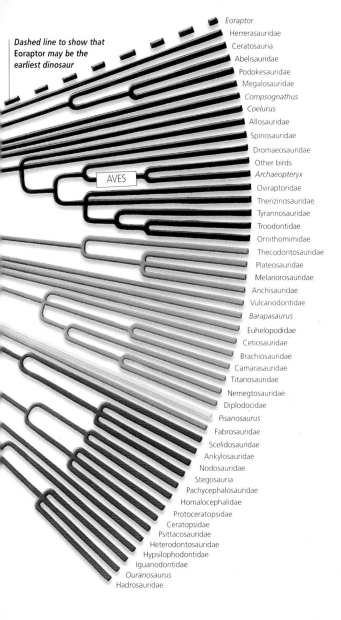

Dashed line to show that Eoraptor may be the earliest dinosaur

Eoraptor
Herrerasauridae
Ceratosauria
Abelisauridae
Podokesauridae
Megalosauridae
Compsognathus
Coelurus
Allosauridae
Spinosauridae
Dromaeosauridae
Other birds
Archaeopteryx
Oviraptoridae
Therizinosauridae
Tyrannosauridae
Troodontidae
Ornithomimidae
Thecodontosauridae
Plateosauridae
Melanorosauridae
Anchisauridae
Vulcanodontidae
Barapasaurus
Euhelopodidae
Cetiosauridae
Brachiosauridae
Camarasauridae
Titanosauridae
Nemegtosauridae
Diplodocidae
Pisanosaurus
Fabrosauridae
Scelidosauridae
Ankylosauridae
Nodosauridae
Stegosauria
Pachycephalosauridae
Homalocephalidae
Protoceratopsidae
Ceratopsidae
Psittacosauridae
Heterodontosauridae
Hypsilophodontidae
Iguanodontidae
Ouranosaurus
Hadrosauridae

AVES

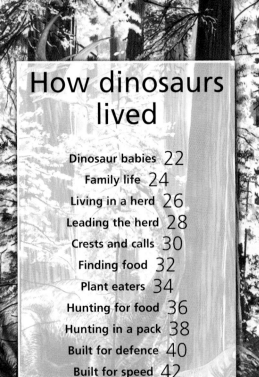

How dinosaurs lived

A giant hunter, *Megalosaurus*, stalks a herd of *Camptosaurus* during the Jurassic Period, 170 million years ago.

Dinosaur babies

Some dinosaurs laid their eggs then left them to hatch by themselves. Other dinosaurs stayed with their eggs to protect them and the babies when they hatched.

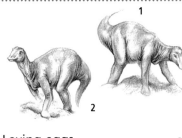

1

2

Maiasaura laying eggs

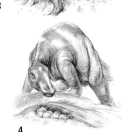

Laying eggs

3

Maiasaura, a duckbilled dinosaur, returned to the same nesting ground each year. Each mother made a mound of sand and earth (1) then scooped a shallow hole in the middle (2). She laid about 20 eggs (3) then covered them with sand or plants to keep them safe and warm (4).

4

Maiasaura *hatchlings each about 35 cm (14 in) long*

Maiasaura babies hatching from eggs

Staying with mother

Some dinosaur babies may have left their nest as soon as they hatched and would have been able to take care of themselves. Other babies were looked after by their mother. She probably brought them food until they were strong enough to find their own.

Lambeosaurus **and her young**

Dinosaur eggs

Just like a bird's egg, each dinosaur egg contained the baby animal and a yolk, or food supply. The growing baby was surrounded by a thin stretchy covering, called a membrane, and protected by a leathery shell. The dinosaur grew in the egg until it was large enough to hatch out and live in the open air.

Duckbill's egg, 18–20 cm (7–8 in) long

Hen's egg, 6 cm (2 in) long

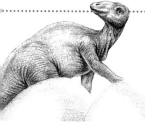

Hatching out

A dinosaur hatchling may have had a small horn on its nose to help it break out of its egg, rather like the egg tooth of a chick. The horn would have fallen off after a few days.

23

Family life

In 1978, a *Maiasaura* nesting site was discovered in Montana, in the United States. It contained an adult, several youngsters, hatchlings and eggs. It indicated to scientists that some dinosaurs were social animals and lived in families.

Maiasaura youngsters

Maiasaura babies probably stayed in their nest for a few months. As they grew bigger and stronger, their mother probably led them from the nest so they could learn to find food for themselves.

Egg thieves

Eggs and baby dinosaurs were helpless, so they were always in danger of being grabbed by hungry predators looking for an easy meal. Adults had to guard their nesting sites from fast-moving meat eaters, such as *Troodon* or *Velociraptor*.

Troodon stealing an egg from an *Edmontosaurus* nest

Staying safe

Some youngsters may have stayed with their mother for several years until they were fully grown. Others grew up and lived in a herd with hundreds of other animals. Large herds helped to keep youngsters safe from attack.

Camarasaurus mother and baby

Modern mothers

Studying animals alive today helps scientists understand how the dinosaurs lived. Although most reptiles leave their hatchlings to look after themselves, crocodiles guard their nests and help their babies hatch from their eggs.

Mother crocodile carrying babies in her mouth

25

Living in a Herd

Living in a herd was safer for many kinds of dinosaur just as it is for animals today. Together, the dinosaurs could warn one another of an approaching predator or other dangers.

Safety on the Move

Some dinosaurs, such as *Apatosaurus* and *Iguanodon*, travelled hundreds of kilometres (miles) to find new sources of food. As they migrated from one feeding ground to another, younger dinosaurs travelled in the middle of the herd, guarded by larger adults.

Herd of migrating long-necked dinosaurs

More experienced adults protecting smaller, younger dinosaurs

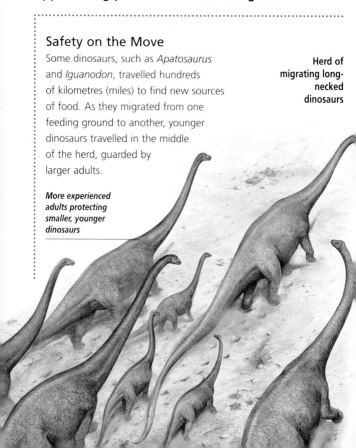

Attacking a Herd

Some meat eaters may have followed a large herd, waiting to pick off a weaker member that dropped behind or became separated from the rest of the group. A big plant eater would have provided enough food to keep a large meat eater satisfied for several days, so the other animals in the herd would be safe until that particular predator went hunting again.

Albertosaurus trying to attack a herd of Triceratops

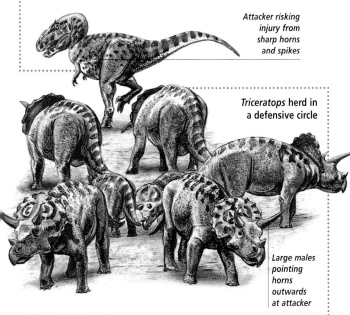

Attacker risking injury from sharp horns and spikes

Triceratops herd in a defensive circle

Large males pointing horns outwards at attacker

Safety in Numbers

When attacked, some peaceful plant eaters would back into a defensive circle around younger and weaker members of the herd. In this way, horned dinosaurs such as Triceratops would present their attacker with a wall of spiky horns and the meat eater would hopefully look for an easier meal elsewhere.

Leading the herd

At the start of the breeding season, some male dinosaurs may have fought one another to win mates and decide which animal would lead the herd, just like rams or deer do today.

Boneheads

Some dinosaurs, such as *Stegoceras,* had domes of thick bone on top of their skulls. Male boneheads had much bigger domes than females, and their domes grew larger as the animals grew older. Some boneheaded dinosaurs also had bony frills and knobs on the back and sides of their heads, and sometimes on their snouts.

Skull protected by thick dome of bone

Stegoceras skull

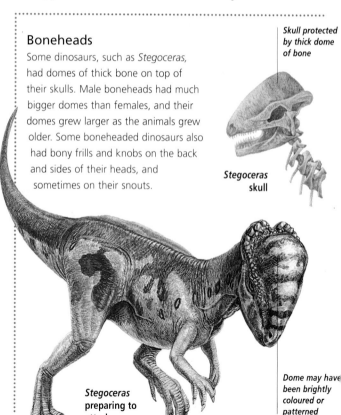

Dome may have been brightly coloured or patterned

Stegoceras preparing to attack

Head to head

Male boneheads fought by lowering their heads, raising their tails for balance and charging at each other until their heads crashed together. They would probably do this over and over again until the weaker animal ran away.

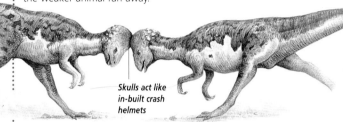

Skulls act like in-built crash helmets

Rival *Pachycephalosaurus* males in a head-on clash

Keep away!

Many horned dinosaurs had sheets of bone, called frills, growing from the backs of their skulls. Long horns and large frills helped to protect the dinosaur if it was attacked by a meat eater, but they may also have helped the animal win the leadership of the herd.

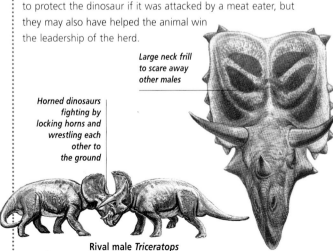

Large neck frill to scare away other males

Horned dinosaurs fighting by locking horns and wrestling each other to the ground

Rival male *Triceratops*

Male *Chasmosaurus*

29

Crests and calls

Duckbilled dinosaurs, named because of their ducklike beaks, lived in huge herds. Many types of duckbill also had crests, which may have been used to hoot or honk.

Different crests

Herds of different kinds of duckbilled dinosaurs lived in the same areas, browsing peacefully on plants. Their various crests and calls may have helped them to recognise and keep in touch with members of the same herd, as well as to find a mate. Males of the same species may have had larger crests than the females.

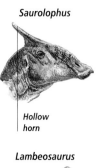

Saurolophus

Edmontosaurus

Parasaurolophus male with long, hollow crest

Hollow horn

Nose flap could be inflated to make honking sounds

Lambeosaurus

Corythosaurus

Bony axe-shaped crest

Dome-shaped crest

Duckbilled dinosaurs

Duckbills were the most common and varied group of dinosaurs. By the Late Cretaceous Period, they had spread all over the northern part of the Earth. They were bulky animals. The largest, *Shantungosaurus*, was about 13 metres (43 feet) long.

Left to right: Corythosaurus, Edmontosaurus and Shantungosaurus

Calling out

If a large meat eater approached, *Parasaurolophus* could make loud honking noises. These sounds would echo through the forest, warning other members of the herd of danger so that they had time to escape.

Inside a crest

Air space

Nose bone

Inside the crest

The curved tubes inside the crest ran from the nose bone. They were probably used as sounding tubes, like the curved tubes of a trumpet.

Finding food

Like animals today, dinosaurs would have spent a lot of time finding enough food to keep themselves alive. The herbivores ate plants. The carnivores ate the herbivores and smaller meat eaters.

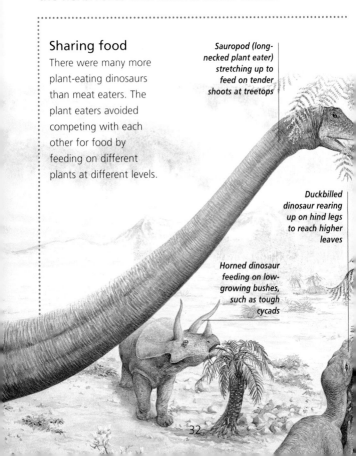

Sharing food

There were many more plant-eating dinosaurs than meat eaters. The plant eaters avoided competing with each other for food by feeding on different plants at different levels.

Sauropod (long-necked plant eater) stretching up to feed on tender shoots at treetops

Duckbilled dinosaur rearing up on hind legs to reach higher leaves

Horned dinosaur feeding on low-growing bushes, such as tough cycads

Teeth for the job

Different types of plant eaters evolved different mouthparts and teeth to deal with different types of vegetation, from tender shoots to tough pinecones and stringy ferns.

Stumpy, peglike teeth to strip tender shoots and leaves from trees

Camarasaurus (a sauropod)

Flat teeth at back to grind hard, crunchy pinecones

Edmontosaurus (a duckbill)

Triceratops (a horned dinosaur)

Sharp, pointed beak and teeth to chop tough ferns

Meat eaters

Large meat eaters hunted or scavenged (ate animals already dead) for their food. They had wide, powerful jaws lined with daggerlike teeth. The teeth curved backwards and had sawlike edges to slice through flesh and bone.

Allosaurus (a meat eater)

Pointed teeth with sawlike edges to stab and tear flesh

Plant eaters

Plant food is more difficult to digest than meat, so plant-eating dinosaurs needed larger stomachs and guts than the meat eaters. This meant that they had bigger bodies than the meat eaters, too.

Biggest plant eaters

The biggest plant eaters – and the largest land animals ever to have lived on the Earth – were the long-necked sauropods. One of these giants probably munched its way through 230 kilograms (507 pounds) of vegetation a day to feed its bulky body.

Long-necked Cetiosaurus feeding on high branches

Feeding habits

Plant eaters such as *Iguanodon* and *Stegosaurus* would have spent most of their time on all fours, browsing on low-growing plants. But they could also rear up on their hind legs to feed.

Stegosaurus rearing up on its hind legs to reach higher-growing branches

Gastroliths stayed in the stomach, mashing tough vegetation into a mushy paste.

Stomach stones

To help them digest tough plant food, the sauropods sometimes swallowed stones, called gastroliths. The stones helped to break down food in the stomach so that it could be absorbed into the body more easily.

Brachiosaurs

The brachiosaurs were the biggest of the sauropods. *Brachiosaurus* weighed up to 80 tonnes (78 tons). Camarasaurs were smaller, with shorter necks and tails.

Brachiosaurus (right) and Camarasaurus – common during the late Jurassic Period

Hunting for food

Some meat-eating dinosaurs hunted alone, stalking and killing their prey. Many meat eaters may have been scavengers, feeding on the remains of animals that were already dead.

Tyrannosaurus

Tyrannosaurus lived during the Cretaceous Period and fed mostly on duckbilled dinosaurs, such as *Edmontosaurus*. Some scientists think that *Tyrannosaurus* and other large meat eaters were too big and clumsy to run fast and hunt their prey. Instead, they may have scavenged for their food. Other scientists believe that *Tyrannosaurus* was an active hunter. Probably, they were both hunters and scavengers.

Tyrannosaurus hunting a herd of duckbills

Speedy hunter

Ornitholestes was a lightly built, fast hunter which preyed on smaller animals, such as lizards, frogs and flying insects.

Slender, clawed hands to grasp prey

Bigger and fiercer

For a long time, people thought that *Tyrannosaurus* was the biggest meat-eating dinosaur. Now scientists have found the remains of even larger carnivores – *Giganotosaurus* and *Carcharodontosaurus*.

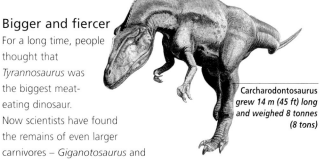

Carcharodontosaurus *grew 14 m (45 ft) long and weighed 8 tonnes (8 tons)*

Carcharodontosaurus

A mouth of knives

Tyrannosaurus had a mouth large enough to swallow you whole! Its jaws were hinged with a thick band of muscle that opened them nearly 90 centimetres (3 feet) wide. Inside were about 60 razor-sharp teeth, each as long as a steak knife.

Pointed teeth each about 15 cm (6 in) long

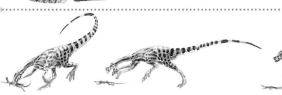

Ornitholestes probably held its tail out for balance as it ran.

Hunting in a pack

Killing a massive plant eater would be difficult even for a big meat eater, but smaller dinosaurs hunting in a pack could attack and kill a much larger animal than themselves.

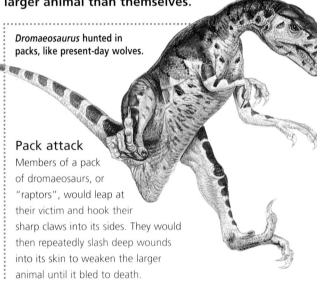

Dromaeosaurus hunted in packs, like present-day wolves.

Pack attack

Members of a pack of dromaeosaurs, or "raptors", would leap at their victim and hook their sharp claws into its sides. They would then repeatedly slash deep wounds into its skin to weaken the larger animal until it bled to death.

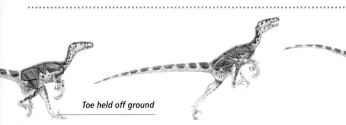

Toe held off ground

Dromaeosaurus leaped on its prey's back or stood on one foot and kicked it.

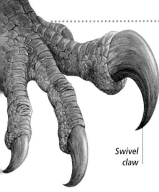

Terrible claw

The hooklike claw on the second toe of a dromaeosaur's foot was a lethal weapon. As a dromaeosaur leaped at its prey, its toe claws swivelled round to slash and hack at its victim. Perhaps dromaeosaurs and other raptors kept their claws razor sharp by raking them against trees, as cats do today.

Swivel claw

Dromaeosaurus foot

Deinonychus had a large head and powerful jaws.

Clever hunter

At 3–4 metres (10–13 feet) long and 2 metres (6½ feet) tall, *Deinonychus* was twice as big as *Dromaeosaurus*. Scientists think it had a large brain for its size, making it cleverer than many plant-eating dinosaurs of its day. It probably also had good hearing and eyesight – essential for a hunter.

Fast killer

Dromaeosaurus may have been able to sprint at over 60 kilometres per hour (37 miles an hour). When it ran, it held its huge toe claws clear of the ground.

39

Built for defence

Towards the end of the Cretaceous Period, some plant eaters evolved armour of horns, spikes and shields to protect themselves against fierce predators.

Single long horn

Big horn

Like other large horned dinosaurs, *Centrosaurus* may have recognised members of its herd by the shape and size of their neck frills and number of horns. The best-known horned dinosaur is *Triceratops*, meaning "three-horned face".

Neck frill with two small curved horns and jagged edges

Centrosaurus

Long spearlike central horn

Big head

A big horned dinosaur was about the size of a present-day rhinoceros. It had a powerful body and muscular legs to support the weight of its heavy horns and neck frill. Heads and horns may have been patterned with bold swirls and stripes.

Styracosaurus

Frill with spiked horns

Plated dinosaurs

The stegosaurs were plated dinosaurs. The double row of pointed plates on their backs may have been used as armour or to keep the dinosaurs cool. Some stegosaurs also had spiked tails.

***Stegosaurus* defending itself against an attacker**

Shoulder spikes

Sauropelta

The armoured dinosaurs had bony plates and studs all over their backs. Some had spikes sticking out of their shoulders or sides. If attacked, they would crouch down to protect their softer underbellies, leaving their attacker with a mouthful of bone.

Spikes to scare away or wound an attacker

Tail clubs

Some armoured dinosaurs had large bones at the end of their tails. They probably used these as clubs. The blow from a tail club may have been powerful enough to break an attacker's legs.

Bony plates and spikes

Tail held out straight, like a club

Euoplocephalus

Built for speed

Some dinosaurs did not have horns and armour to defend themselves. Instead, they were extremely fast runners. They used their speed to hunt smaller prey and to escape from hungry predators.

Ostrichlike dinosaurs

Gallimimus, *Struthiomimus* and *Ornithomimus* belonged to a group of dinosaurs called ornithomimids. They had narrow beaks and long back legs and looked like present-day ostriches. Their large eyes and brains made them efficient hunters, but they probably ate fruit and berries as well as insects and other small animals.

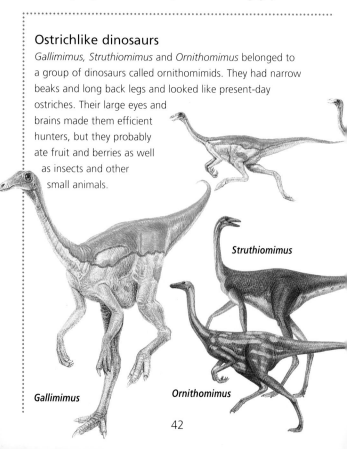

Struthiomimus

Gallimimus

Ornithomimus

42

Fast hunters

Although the ornithomimids were probably the fastest dinosaurs, other theropods could also run quickly. Some scientists believe that even bulky tyrannosaurs and allosaurs could have managed short bursts of speed up to 40 kilometres an hour (25 miles per hour).

Gasosaurus running to attack *Huayangosaurus*, a plated dinosaur

Gallimimus ran on its long back legs, holding out its tail for balance.

Long legs

The ornithomimids had strong thigh muscles and long bones in their back legs. They also had light, slender ankle bones. These helped to push them forwards so that they could run fast. *Gallimimus* was about 4 metres (13 feet) long – about twice the size of a modern ostrich. It could probably sprint at up to 64 kilometres an hour (40 miles per hour).

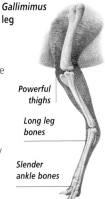

Gallimimus leg

Powerful thighs

Long leg bones

Slender ankle bones

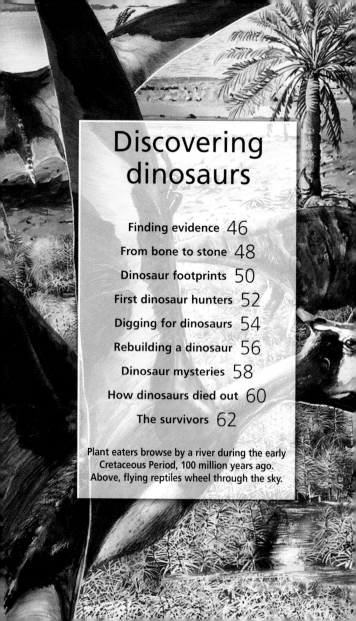

Discovering dinosaurs

Plant eaters browse by a river during the early
Cretaceous Period, 100 million years ago.
Above, flying reptiles wheel through the sky.

Finding evidence

The dinosaurs died out 65 million years ago, long before they could be seen and studied by a human being. We only know about the dinosaurs because of the clues they left behind.

Dinosaur remains

Fossilised bones are the main evidence that the dinosaurs existed. It is rare to find a complete dinosaur skeleton. Bones are often missing or jumbled together. Sometimes, the remains of different dinosaurs are found in the same place – for example, the fossilised teeth of a meat eater among the bones of a plant eater. The meat eater probably lost its teeth while it was scavenging for food.

Reconstructed skeleton of a horned dinosaur

Iguanodon **leg bone**

Muscle marks

Fossilised bones have rough marks where muscles were attached. Scientists compare these with the bones of living animals to help them reconstruct the shape of a dinosaur's body.

46

Living dinosaurs

Dinosaurs were living, breathing
creatures. They had to find food,
protect themselves from danger,
and raise their young – just like
animals today. This means they
may have looked like some
present-day reptiles and
mammals, and may have
behaved in similar ways.
For example, a bulky, long-
necked plant eater may have
had a similar lifestyle to a
present-day giraffe.

**Long-necked Brachiosaurus
probably stretched its head
up to the treetops to feed,
as does a present-day giraffe.**

*Brachiosaurus had
a similar neck and
head structure
to a giraffe*

Long neck

*Broad,
powerful
shoulders*

From bone to stone

Most animals live and die without leaving any permanent trace of their existence. But occasionally, if conditions are suitable, an animal becomes fossilised. We only know dinosaurs existed because of their fossilised remains.

How a fossil forms

Imagine a dinosaur dies by the bank of a muddy lake. Its flesh is eaten or rots away. As the years pass, the skeleton sinks. Minerals slowly turn the soft surrounding mud into hard rock. They also replace the minerals in the bones of the skeleton, turning them into stone.

Flesh is eaten by scavengers or rots away

Skeleton sinks into mud of lake

Knobbly skin impression from an armoured dinosaur

Skin prints

Skin was usually eaten, or rotted away with a dinosaur's other soft body parts. But occasionally, scientists find rocks with the impression, or prints, of dinosaur skin.

Fossilised teeth

Teeth are covered with a
layer of hard enamel and
because of this survive well as
fossils. Dinosaur teeth can tell
scientists a lot about their owner.
Meat eaters have long, pointed teeth.
Plant eaters have many smaller teeth
for grinding down food.

**Fossilised tooth
of a meat eater**

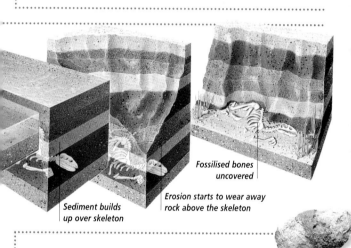

*Sediment builds
up over skeleton*

*Erosion starts to wear away
rock above the skeleton*

*Fossilised bones
uncovered*

Other fossils

Scientists have found many fossilised dinosaur
eggs. Some even contain small skeletons. Eggs
are sometimes found in nests, complete with
the fossils of young dinosaurs. Scientists even
occasionally find fossilised dinosaur droppings,
called coprolites.

**Droppings can
tell us what
dinosaurs ate**

**Fossilised
eggs**

Dinosaur footprints

Dinosaur footprints can tell us a lot about dinosaurs and how they lived. From dinosaur tracks, we know whether a dinosaur walked on two legs or on all fours, how fast it moved, and whether it travelled in herds.

Forming footprints

Imagine a dinosaur walks across muddy land near a river or a lake and that the mud dries quickly, baking hard in the sun. Millions of years later, erosion may strip away the softer layers of mud and sand that have built up over the footprints and expose them once more.

Dinosaur footprints preserved in rock

Camarasaurus moved slowly while *Gallimimus* was a fast runner.

Camarasaurus

Telltale tracks

Scientists do not know for sure which dinosaur made which tracks. However, they can make a reasonable guess by comparing the size and shape of footprints with the feet of dinosaurs known to have lived in the area when the footprints were made. They can tell how old the footprints are by working out the age of the rocks in which they are found.

Palaeontologist examining tracks

Megalosaurus

Iguanodon

Iguanodon moved on all four legs and *Megalosaurus* on two.

How fast were they?

Scientists can work out how fast a dinosaur travelled by the length of its legs and the distance between its footprints. The faster a dinosaur moved, the greater the spaces between the footprints.

Gallimimus

First dinosaur hunters

The French scientist Georges Cuvier was the first person to realise, around 200 years ago, that some fossil remains were so unusual that they must belong to creatures no longer living on the Earth.

"Iguana tooth"

Gideon Mantell's sketch of an *Iguanodon*

In 1820, a British doctor called Gideon Mantell found some fossilised teeth. He thought they belonged to an extinct relative of the iguana lizard, and named the new animal *Iguanodon*, meaning "iguana tooth".

Dinosaur statues were built in 1854 following the ideas of Richard Owen; the statues now stand in Crystal Palace Park, London.

Dinosauria

In 1842, British palaeontologist Richard Owen realised that the remains of *Iguanodon* and other large reptiles must belong to a separate group of creatures, which he named dinosauria, or "terrible lizards". All over the world, people became fascinated by the dinosaurs and tried to discover more of their remains.

Bone Wars

In the United States, a race to discover the most dinosaur fossils developed between Edward Drinker Cope, a scientist and fossil collector, and Othniel Charles Marsh, professor of palaeontology at Yale University. Cope and Marsh did not like each other and each hired armed workers to steal the other's finds.

Above: Cope discovered (among others) *Camarasaurus* and *Coelophysis*. Left: Marsh (back row, centre) discovered *Stegosaurus* and *Allosaurus*.

Barnum Brown

In the early 20th century, Barnum Brown of the American Museum of Natural History in New York found the remains of many duckbilled and horned dinosaurs in Canada. His success encouraged the museum to send expeditions to the Gobi Desert in central Asia, where more dinosaur remains were found.

Barnum Brown (right) on his 1911 expedition to Red Deer River in Alberta, Canada

Digging for dinosaurs

Dinosaur fossils are sometimes found by accident. More often, they are discovered by members of scientific expeditions, who know in which types and ages of rock to look.

Finding fossils

Since the days of Cope and Marsh, dinosaur hunting has spread all over the world. Hunting for fossils takes time and money. Some trips take years to plan. Today's palaeontologists usually set out on specific expeditions, to places where they know fossils to be common.

Palaeontologists working on a tyrannosaur skull

Unearthing a skeleton

Once a skeleton has been found, the first job is to get it under cover. After lying in the ground for millions of years, the bones are usually cracked and delicate. First, the rock lying above the bones is carefully removed. Then pieces of rock surrounding the bones are cut out of the ground. Each piece of rock is wrapped in strips of cloth soaked in plaster of Paris to protect it.

Freeing a skeleton from rock takes a team of people, working with such tools as pneumatic drills, pickaxes and soft brushes.

54

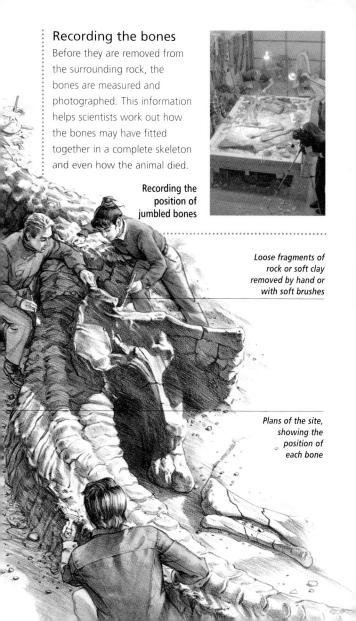

Recording the bones

Before they are removed from the surrounding rock, the bones are measured and photographed. This information helps scientists work out how the bones may have fitted together in a complete skeleton and even how the animal died.

Recording the position of jumbled bones

Loose fragments of rock or soft clay removed by hand or with soft brushes

Plans of the site, showing the position of each bone

Rebuilding a dinosaur

Before a dinosaur skeleton can be studied and possibly reconstructed, each bone must be cleaned and preserved. This work is done by experts in a laboratory. Sometimes it may take years to prepare a whole skeleton.

Preparator removing rock from bone

Cleaning the bones

Preparators use different tools to remove rock from bones. Soft rock is usually chipped away with chisels and knives. Harder rock may be drilled away by a hand-held tool rather like a dentist's drill. Bones are usually dark brown, so it is easy to tell rock from bone.

Reconstructing a skeleton

Scientists may make plaster casts or fibreglass models of bones, particularly if the bones are rare or in good condition. These may be used in museum exhibits, or they may be exchanged with different bones from another museum. If a skeleton is incomplete, scientists make models of the missing bones. They base these on the skeletons of other, similar dinosaurs.

Museum display of *Albertosaurus* and *Centrosaurus* skeletons in front of an artist's painting of how the dinosaurs may have looked during the Cretaceous Period

Putting it together

Palaeontologists study each bone of a dinosaur in great detail to work out how its skeleton fits together. They then make drawings to show how muscles probably moved the bones, using evidence from the surface of each bone and comparisons with similar, present-day animals. Once they have a good idea of the shape and size of a dinosaur, they can imagine what it looked like when the muscle was covered with skin. They must also decide whether the animal had horny claws, feathers or lips – body parts that do not fossilise easily – and what colour it may have been.

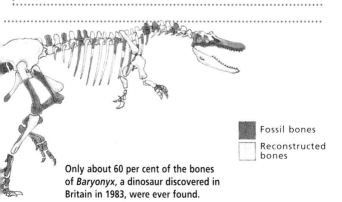

■ Fossil bones
□ Reconstructed bones

Only about 60 per cent of the bones of *Baryonyx*, a dinosaur discovered in Britain in 1983, were ever found.

Dinosaur mysteries

Although we know a lot about dinosaurs, there is much that we do not understand. New species of dinosaur are being discovered all the time. These discoveries may change our views of current finds.

A fish-eating dinosaur?

The remains of an unusual dinosaur, named *Baryonyx*, were discovered in Sussex, England, in 1983. The skeleton was incomplete, but its skull had a long pointed snout and outward-pointing teeth. *Baryonyx* also had a large curved claw, nearly 30 centimetres (12 inches) long. Some scientists think *Baryonyx* was well adapted to hunting fish, but no one knows for sure.

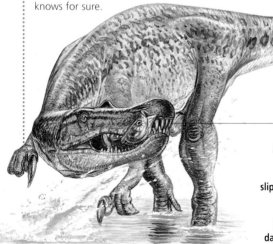

Large teeth pointing forward

***Baryonyx* may have speared and grasped slippery fish with its long claws and jaws, just like a present-day grizzly bear.**

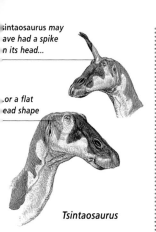

sintaosaurus may ave had a spike n its head...

.or a flat ead shape

Tsintaosaurus

Horn or no horn?

Some experts think the duckbilled dinosaur *Tsintaosaurus* had a spike on its head. Others believe the spike is actually a displaced bone from the animal's skull and that it had a flat head shape.

Single claw

Experts still do not agree about dinosaurs grouped into a family called the alvarezsaurs, or "single claws". Some scientists think they may have been early birds because their skeletons are similar to those of birds. Others think they were a kind of meat-eating dinosaur. No one knows how they used their strange, short arms.

Mononykus had short, stumpy arms.

Modern lizards are cold-blooded. But were the dinosaurs, too?

Warm-blooded or cold-blooded?

Scientists still do not know for sure whether the dinosaurs were warm- or cold-blooded. Warm-blooded animals can control their own body temperature. Cold-blooded animals rely on heat from the Sun to increase their body temperature and warm them.

59

How dinosaurs died out

Dinosaurs became extinct at the end of the Cretaceous Period, 65 million years ago. Because this happened so long ago, scientists are not sure whether this extinction took place over thousands of years or over one hundred years.

What went wrong?

Some scientists think that dinosaurs were slowly becoming fewer and less varied for several million years before they finally became extinct. There is also evidence that a huge meteorite struck Earth during the late Cretaceous Period, changing Earth's climate and killing many creatures in a mass extinction.

After a meteorite hit the Earth, plants would have died from lack of sunlight, then the plant eaters would have died, and then the meat eaters that fed on them.

Changing climate

The impact from a huge meteorite hitting the Earth would have sent up a cloud of rock and dust into the atmosphere, blocking out the Sun's light and warmth and cooling the Earth's climate.

The impact site

A huge crater has been found near the north coast of Mexico. This could have been made by a meteorite striking the Earth during the Cretaceous Period. The impact would have caused tidal waves and earthquakes as well as clouds of dust.

Possible impact site

Yucatán

MEXICO

The Yucatán area of Mexico may have been the site of the meteorite impact.

Size of the crater

The hole made by the meteorite was about 100 kilometres (60 miles) wide and 12 kilometres (7 miles) deep. The dark blue area at the bottom of this image shows a trench blasted out by the meteorite as it approached.

Computer-generated image of the crater

The survivors

By the end of the Cretaceous Period, all the dinosaurs, pterosaurs, ichthyosaurs and plesiosaurs had become extinct, but many other animals survived.

Who survived?

Turtles, mammals, lizards, snakes, crocodiles, birds and many insects all survived beyond the Cretaceous Period. The extinction of the dinosaurs left a gap for other large animals to fill. Mammals became bigger and more varied until they were the most common large animals on the Earth. Dinosaurs will never rule the Earth again, but their descendants – birds – live on.

PERMIAN 290–250 MYA	TRIASSIC 250–205 MYA	JURASSIC 205–140 MYA	

Toothed beak (unlike modern birds which do not have teeth)

Closest-living relatives

Like a dinosaur, *Archaeopteryx* had teeth, clawed fingers and a long, bony tail. It also had feathers on its wings and tail like those of a bird. For many years people thought that *Archaeopteryx* was the best proof that birds evolved from dinosaurs. Then, in the late 1990s, scientists discovered the remains of similar half-bird, half-dinosaur creatures in China. Today, most scientists agree that birds are the dinosaurs' closest-living relatives.

Archaeopteryx could fly but probably had to climb trees to launch itself into the air.

TACEOUS 0–65 MYA	CENOZOIC 65 MYA–PRESENT DAY
	TORTOISES/TURTLES
	MAMMALS
ICHTHYOSAURS	
PLESIOSAURS	
	LIZARDS
	SNAKES
	CROCODILES
PTEROSAURS	
ORNITHISCHIAN DINOSAURS	
SAURISCHIAN DINOSAURS	
	BIRDS

Guide to dinosaurs

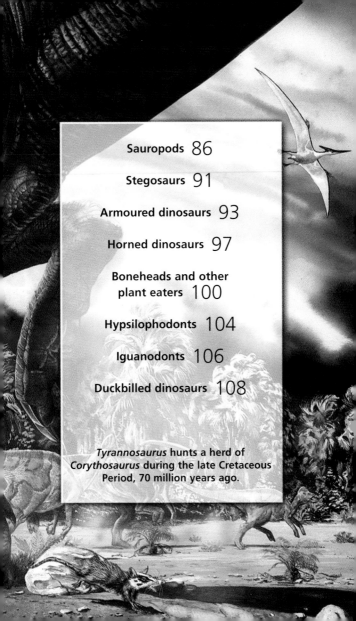

Tyrannosaurus hunts a herd of
Corythosaurus during the late Cretaceous
Period, 70 million years ago.

First dinosaurs

Eoraptor and *Herrerasaurus* are the earliest dinosaurs we know about. They lived 228 million years ago, during the Triassic Period.

EORAPTOR
(EE-oh-RAP-tor)

Family:	Theropoda?
Size:	1 m (3¼ ft) long
Food:	Meat, maybe insects
Period:	Late Triassic
Range:	South America: northwestern Argentina

Eoraptor, named in 1993, means "dawn thief" because it hunted for food at the beginning, or dawn of the Age of Dinosaurs. It had short front legs and probably ran on its longer hind legs.

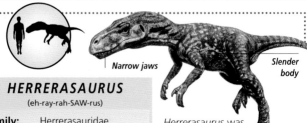

Narrow jaws

Slender body

HERRERASAURUS
(eh-ray-rah-SAW-rus)

Family:	Herrerasauridae
Size:	3–6 m (10–20 ft) long
Food:	Meat, such as lizards
Period:	Late Triassic
Range:	South America: northwestern Argentina

Herrerasaurus was named after its discoverer, Victorino Herrera. It had large jaws and may have swallowed its prey whole. Like *Eoraptor*, it stood upright on its hind legs.

Ceratosaurs

Ceratosaurs were meat eaters. The group includes about 20 dinosaurs, ranging from small *Coelophysis* to huge *Dilophosaurus*.

COMPSOGNATHUS

(komp-soh-NAY-thus)

Family:	Compsognathidae
Size:	60 cm (2 ft) long
Food:	Meat
Period:	Late Jurassic
Range:	Europe: France, Germany

Compsognathus was about the size of a present-day chicken. It probably darted through the undergrowth, hunting small lizards.

COELOPHYSIS

(seel-oh-FY-sis)

Family:	Podokesauridae
Size:	3 m (10 ft) long
Food:	Meat
Period:	Late Triassic
Range:	North America: New Mexico, Connecticut

Coelophysis was built for speed, with long back legs and a lightweight body. It had a long tail, which it may have held out for balance as it ran. It may have hunted in packs.

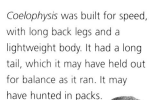

Leg bones were hollow to make them lighter

Dilophosaurus (meaning "two-crested lizard") was one of the first large meat-eating dinosaurs. It had a slim, lightweight body and slender jaws lined with sharp teeth. Its crest may have been used for signalling.

DILOPHOSAURUS
(die-LOAF-oh-SAW-rus)

Family:	Ceratosauridae
Size:	6 m (20 ft) long
Food:	Meat
Period:	Early Jurassic
Range:	North America: Arizona; Antarctica

Ceratosaurus ("horned reptile") was a large dinosaur with huge fangs. The horn on its nose may have been used for display, to warn away males of the same species and win a mate.

CERATOSAURUS
(SER-a-toe-SAW-rus)

Family:	Ceratosauridae
Size:	6 m (20 ft) long
Food:	Meat
Period:	Late Jurassic
Range:	Africa: Tanzania; North America: Colorado, Wyoming

Heavy jaws with long, curved fangs

Tetanurans

The tetanurans were a group of large, fierce meat eaters that lived during the Jurassic and Cretaceous periods. They included allosaurs, spinosaurs and megalosaurs.

The skeleton of *Giganotosaurus* ("gigantic southern lizard") *was* discovered in South America in 1993. It was as heavy as *Tyrannosaurus*, weighing around 8 tonnes (8 tons), but was more closely related to *Allosaurus* of the Jurassic Period.

GIGANOTOSAURUS
(JI-gan-o-toe-SAW-rus)

Family:	Abelisauridae
Size:	13 m (43 ft) long
Food:	Meat, maybe animals already dead
Period:	Late Cretaceous
Range:	South America: Patagonia

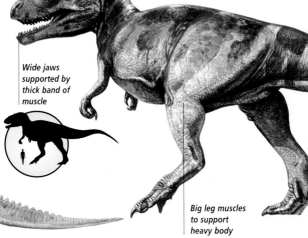

Wide jaws supported by thick band of muscle

Big leg muscles to support heavy body

Ridges on skull running from eyes to tip of snout

Three-fingered hands

ALLOSAURUS
(AL-oh-SAW-rus)

Family:	Allosauridae
Size:	Up to 12 m (40 ft) long
Food:	Meat: other dinosaurs
Period:	Late Jurassic
Range:	Africa: Tanzania; North America: Colorado, Utah, Wyoming; Australia

Allosaurus ("foreign reptile") was the main large meat-eating dinosaur of North America during the late Jurassic Period. It had a large head and a strong neck. Its powerful jaws were lined with more than 70 teeth.

CRYOLOPHOSAURUS
(cry-oh-LOAF-oh-SAW-rus)

Family:	Uncertain
Size:	7–8 m (23–26 ft) long
Food:	Meat
Period:	Early Jurassic
Range:	Antarctica

Cryolophosaurus (meaning "cold crested lizard") was discovered in 1991, in Antarctica. It had a thin, bony crest rising up in a ridge across its skull. The crest may have been covered with brightly coloured skin.

Megalosaurus ("great reptile") was the first dinosaur to be named, in 1824. It had long, curved teeth with jagged front and back edges. Each of the four toes on its feet ended in a long claw.

MEGALOSAURUS
(MEG-ah-loh-SAW-rus)

Family:	Megalosauridae
Size:	9 m (30 ft) long
Food:	Meat
Period:	Jurassic
Range:	Europe: England, France; Africa: Morocco

Yangchuanosaurus was first discovered in China in 1978. It was similar to other allosaurs, with a large head, big jaws and sharp fangs. It had sharp claws on its fingers and toes and held its tail out for balance as it moved.

YANGCHUANOSAURUS
(yang-choo-AN-oh-SAW-rus)

Family:	Allosauridae
Size:	Up to 10 m (33 ft) long
Food:	Meat
Period:	Late Jurassic
Range:	Asia: China

Thick, pillarlike legs

71

CARCHARODONTOSAURUS
(kar-kar-oh-don-toh-SAW-rus)

Family:	Uncertain
Size:	8 m (26 ft) long
Food:	Meat, maybe animals already dead
Period:	Early Cretaceous
Range:	Africa: Egypt, Morocco, Tunisia

Skull measured 1.6 m (5¼ ft) long

Carcharodontosaurus was named after *Carcharodon*, a giant shark. We only have a few of its remains, but these show it to have been a massive creature. Its teeth were 12 cm (5 in) long. It probably fed on the large, plant-eating dinosaurs living in the area at the time.

SPINOSAURUS
(SPINE-oh-SAW-rus)

Family:	Spinosauridae
Size:	12 m (40 ft) long
Food:	Meat
Period:	Late Cretaceous
Range:	Africa: Egypt, Niger, Tunisia

Spinosaurus (meaning "spiny reptile") was named because of the 2-m (6½-ft) tall spines running down the length of its back. These supported a huge, skin-covered sail, or fin, which may have been used to control its body temperature.

72

Bird relatives

The maniraptors included different kinds of birdlike dinosaurs, such as the fearsome dromaeosaurs with curved claws on their toes, as well as birds themselves.

Deinonychus ("terrible claw") was around 4 m (13 ft) long, making it larger than its close relatives *Dromaeosaurus* and *Velociraptor*. It is named after the curved, scythe-like claws on the second toe of each foot. These flicked back as it ran then swivelled down to attack.

DEINONYCHUS
(DIE-noh-NIKE-us)

Family:	Dromaeosauridae
Size:	3–4 m (10–13 ft) long
Food:	Meat: larger dinosaurs
Period:	Early Cretaceous
Range:	North America: Montana

Long jaws lined with jagged teeth to tear flesh

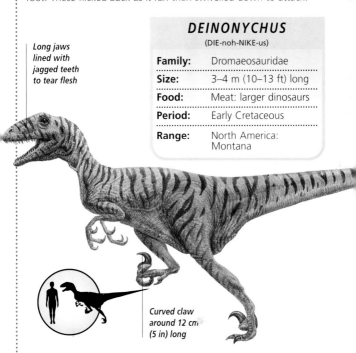

Curved claw around 12 cm (5 in) long

DROMAEOSAURUS
(DROH-may-oh-SAW-rus)

Family:	Dromaeosauridae
Size:	1.8 m (6 ft) long
Food:	Meat
Period:	Late Cretaceous
Range:	North America: Alberta

Long arms to snatch and hold prey

Dromaeosaurus was a small, fast runner, with sharp claws on each foot. It may have eaten turtles, lizards and baby dinosaurs. It was shorter than *Deinonychus* – about the height of a 10-year-old child.

VELOCIRAPTOR
(vel-O-si-RAP-tor)

Family:	Dromaeosauridae
Size:	1.8 m (6 ft) long
Food:	Meat
Period:	Late Cretaceous
Range:	Asia: China, Mongolia

Velociraptor ("fast thief") was a medium-sized, quick hunter. It had a flat snout and long arms. In 1971, scientists found the skeleton of a *Velociraptor* kicking the skeleton of a small horned dinosaur in the belly with its curved toe claw. The two dinosaurs must have died in a fight.

Stenonychosaurus was a slender, fast-running dinosaur. It had large eyes, each about 5 cm (2 in) wide, and may have hunted at night.

STENONYCHOSAURUS
(STEN-oh-nike-o-SAW-rus)

Family:	Troodontidae
Size:	2 m (6½ ft) long
Food:	Meat
Period:	Late Cretaceous
Range:	North America: Alberta

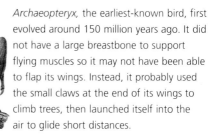

Archaeopteryx, the earliest-known bird, first evolved around 150 million years ago. It did not have a large breastbone to support flying muscles so it may not have been able to flap its wings. Instead, it probably used the small claws at the end of its wings to climb trees, then launched itself into the air to glide short distances.

ARCHAEOPTERYX
(ark-ee-OP-ter-iks)

Family:	Archaeopterygidae, Aves
Size:	35 cm (14 in) long
Food:	Insects, fruit
Period:	Late Jurassic
Range:	Europe: Germany

Ostrich dinosaurs

The ostrichlike dinosaurs, or ornithomimids, looked like featherless ostriches, with long necks, small heads and slender legs.

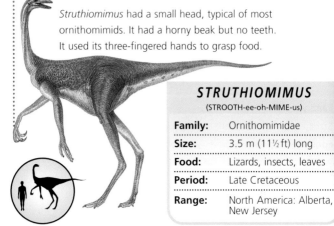

ORNITHOMIMUS
(or-NITH-oh-MIME-us)

Family:	Ornithomimidae
Size:	3.5 m (11½ ft) long
Food:	Lizards, insects, leaves
Period:	Late Cretaceous
Range:	Asia: Tibet; North America: Colorado, Montana

Like other ornithomimids, *Ornithomimus* ("bird mimic") had a long tail that was about half its body length. It would have held its tail out for balance as it ran.

Struthiomimus had a small head, typical of most ornithomimids. It had a horny beak but no teeth. It used its three-fingered hands to grasp food.

STRUTHIOMIMUS
(STROOTH-ee-oh-MIME-us)

Family:	Ornithomimidae
Size:	3.5 m (11½ ft) long
Food:	Lizards, insects, leaves
Period:	Late Cretaceous
Range:	North America: Alberta, New Jersey

Long snout ending in wide, flat beak

Gallimimus ("hen mimic") was the largest ornithomimid, at about twice the size of a modern ostrich. Unlike others in the group, it could not grasp with its hands. Instead, it may have scraped the soil to gather food.

GALLIMIMUS
(gal-lee-MEEM-us)

Family:	Ornithomimidae
Size:	4 m (13 ft) long
Food:	Lizards, insects, leaves, maybe eggs
Period:	Late Cretaceous
Range:	Asia: Mongolia

Dromiceiomimus had long legs and could run fast to escape from danger. It had particularly large eyes, so it may have hunted at night for small mammals and lizards.

DROMICEIOMIMUS
(droh-MEE-see-oh-MEEM-us)

Family:	Ornithomimidae
Size:	3.5 m (11½ ft) long
Food:	Small mammals, lizards, insects, leaves
Period:	Late Cretaceous
Range:	North America: Alberta

ELAPHROSAURUS
(ee-LAF-roe-SAW-rus)

Family:	Ornithomimidae?
Size:	3.5 m (11½ ft) long
Food:	Meat
Period:	Late Jurassic
Range:	Africa: Tanzania

Short arms with three-fingered hands

Scientists think that *Elaphrosaurus* ("light reptile") was an early ostrich dinosaur. It is known from a skeleton found in fossil beds in Tendaguru, Tanzania.

OVIRAPTOR
(OHV-ih-RAP-tor)

Family:	Oviraptoridae
Size:	1.8 m (6 ft) long
Food:	Meat
Period:	Late Cretaceous
Range:	Asia: Mongolia

Oviraptor means "egg thief" because the first *Oviraptor* fossils were discovered in a nest of eggs. At first, scientists thought that the eggs belonged to another dinosaur. Now they know that the eggs were *Oviraptor's* own, and that it probably died protecting them.

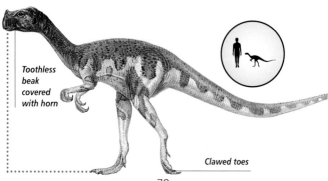

Toothless beak covered with horn

Clawed toes

Tyrannosaurs

The tyrannosaurs were large, fierce meat eaters that lived in Asia and North America during the late Cretaceous Period. They had huge heads and jaws and short, stumpy arms.

Strong jaws lined with long, serrated teeth

TYRANNOSAURUS
(tie-RAN-oh-SAW-rus)

Family:	Tyrannosauridae
Size:	Up to 15 m (50 ft) long
Food:	Meat
Period:	Late Cretaceous
Range:	Asia: Mongolia; North America: Alberta, Montana, Saskatchewan, Texas, Wyoming

Tyrannosaurus is often called by its full name, *Tyrannosaurus rex,* which means "king of the tyrant reptiles". With its short, stumpy front arms and massive head, it is perhaps the most recognisable large, meat-eating dinosaur. *Tyrannosaurus's* arms were too short to reach its mouth when feeding. They may have been used to help the dinosaur lever itself off the ground after sleep.

79

Thick tail held out for balance

ALBERTOSAURUS
(al-BERT-oh-SAW-rus)

Family:	Tyrannosauridae
Size:	8 m (26 ft) long
Food:	Meat: other dinosaurs
Period:	Late Cretaceous
Range:	North America: Alberta, Montana

Albertosaurus, or "lizard from Alberta", was named after the province in Canada in which the first of its remains were found. Like other tyrannosaurs, it may have used its short, stumpy arms to lever itself off the ground after feeding or sleeping.

Tarbosaurus ("reptile from Bataar") was an Asian relative of *Tyrannosaurus*. It may have fed on the duckbilled dinosaurs living in the same area.

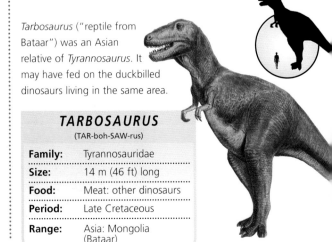

TARBOSAURUS
(TAR-boh-SAW-rus)

Family:	Tyrannosauridae
Size:	14 m (46 ft) long
Food:	Meat: other dinosaurs
Period:	Late Cretaceous
Range:	Asia: Mongolia (Bataar)

Alioramus had a narrower skull than other tyrannosaurs. It also had small, bony lumps on its snout. These may have been used in display, to help attract a mate.

Bony knobs, or spikes

ALIORAMUS
(ay-lee-oh-RAY-mus)

Family:	Tyrannosauridae
Size:	6 m (20 ft) long
Food:	Meat: other dinosaurs
Period:	Late Cretaceous
Range:	Asia: Mongolia

Siamotyrannus was first discovered in Thailand in 1996. Its name means "lizard from Siam", an old name for Thailand. It probably preyed on large, plant-eating dinosaurs living in the same area at the time.

SIAMOTYRANNUS
(sigh-AM-oh-tie-ran-us)

Family:	Tyrannosauridae
Size:	5–7 m (16–23 ft) long
Food:	Meat: other dinosaurs
Period:	Late Cretaceous
Range:	Asia: Thailand

81

Segnosaurs

The segnosaurs, or therizinosaurs, were lightly built meat eaters with long necks and strange sickle-shaped claws on their arms.

THERIZINOSAURUS
(THER-ih-zin-oh-SAW-rus)

Family:	Therizinosauridae
Size:	4–5 m (13–16 ft) long
Food:	Meat, maybe also leaves
Period:	Late Cretaceous
Range:	Asia: China, Mongolia

Therizinosaurus, or "scythe reptile", was named because of its curved claws, each about 70 cm (28 in) long and similar in size and shape to scythes used to cut long grass.

Like *Therizinosaurus*, *Alxasaurus* had a small head and a toothless beak. It may have used its beak to chop up flesh or leaves.

ALXASAURUS
(AHL-shah-SAW-rus)

Family:	Therizinosauridae
Size:	4 m (13 ft) long
Food:	Meat, maybe also leaves
Period:	Late Cretaceous
Range:	Asia: China, Mongolia

Prosauropods

The prosauropods were a group of long-necked dinosaurs that evolved during the late Triassic Period but died out by the end of the early Jurassic Period.

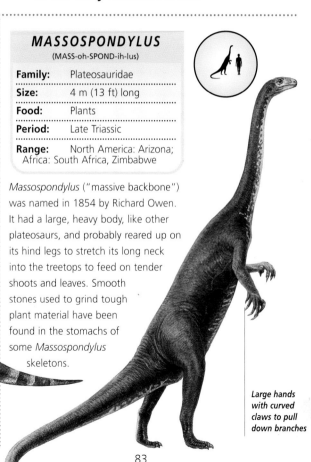

MASSOSPONDYLUS
(MASS-oh-SPOND-ih-lus)

Family:	Plateosauridae
Size:	4 m (13 ft) long
Food:	Plants
Period:	Late Triassic
Range:	North America: Arizona; Africa: South Africa, Zimbabwe

Massospondylus ("massive backbone") was named in 1854 by Richard Owen. It had a large, heavy body, like other plateosaurs, and probably reared up on its hind legs to stretch its long neck into the treetops to feed on tender shoots and leaves. Smooth stones used to grind tough plant material have been found in the stomachs of some *Massospondylus* skeletons.

Large hands with curved claws to pull down branches

83

Young Mussaurus

MUSSAURUS
(moo-SAW-rus)

Family:	Plateosauridae
Size:	3 m (10 ft) long
Food:	Plants
Period:	Late Triassic to Early Jurassic
Range:	South America: Argentina

Mussaurus ("mouse reptile") was named in 1979 after the remains of five or six small skeletons were found in a nest. The largest was the size of a kitten, and the animals were probably youngsters.

RIOJASAURUS
(ree-O-ha-SAW-rus)

Family:	Melanorosauridae
Size:	10 m (33 ft) long
Food:	Plants
Period:	Late Triassic to Early Jurassic
Range:	South America: Argentina

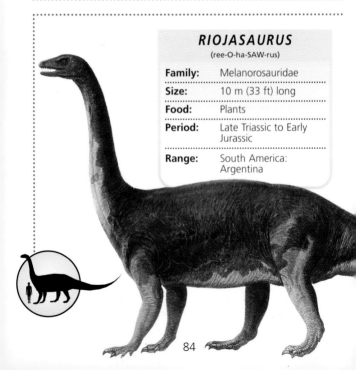

Small head

Large thumb claw to dig up plants

ANCHISAURUS
(AN-ki-SAW-rus)

Family:	Anchisauridae
Size:	2.1 m (7 ft) long
Food:	Plants
Period:	Early Jurassic
Range:	North America: Connecticut; southern Africa

Like other anchisaurs, *Anchisaurus* was a lightly built prosauropod with a small head and a slender body. Its front legs were shorter than its hind legs, and it may have been able to move around on two legs as well as four.

Tail held out to support body weight

Riojasaurus was heavier than *Anchisaurus* and *Massospondylus* and needed to remain on all fours to support its bulky body. It would not have been able to rear up on its hind legs to reach treetop leaves so it would have probably fed on plants growing nearer the ground.

85

Sauropods

The sauropods were long-necked plant eaters that evolved during the Jurassic Period. They are the largest land animals ever to have lived on the Earth.

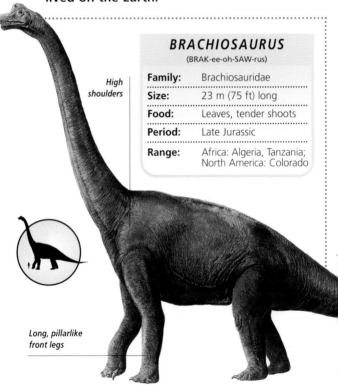

High shoulders

BRACHIOSAURUS
(BRAK-ee-oh-SAW-rus)

Family:	Brachiosauridae
Size:	23 m (75 ft) long
Food:	Leaves, tender shoots
Period:	Late Jurassic
Range:	Africa: Algeria, Tanzania; North America: Colorado

Long, pillarlike front legs

Brachiosaurus was named "arm reptile" because of its long front legs. The shoulders of a *Brachiosaurus* were therefore high above the ground, enabling it to stretch its long neck high into the treetops.

Cetiosaurus ("whale reptile") was named in 1841 from just a few teeth and bones. It was an early sauropod and had a solid backbone. Some of the bones of later sauropods were hollow to reduce weight.

CETIOSAURUS
(SEET-ee-oh-SAW-rus)

Family:	Cetiosauridae
Size:	18.3 m (60 ft) long
Food:	Plants
Period:	Middle to Late Jurassic
Range:	Europe: England; Africa: Morocco

CAMARASAURUS
(kam-AR-a-SAW-rus)

Family:	Camarasauridae
Size:	18.3 m (60 ft) long
Food:	Plants
Period:	Late Jurassic
Range:	North America: Colorado, Utah, Wyoming

Camarasaurus means "chamber lizard", because of the hollows, or chambers, in its backbone. It had a shorter neck than *Diplodocus* or *Brachiosaurus* and a square, boxlike head.

87

SALTASAURUS
(SALT-a-SAW-rus)

Family:	Titanosauridae
Size:	12 m (40 ft) long
Food:	Plants: treetop shoots and leaves
Period:	Late Cretaceous
Range:	South America: Argentina

Saltasaurus (meaning "lizard from Salta", a place in Argentina) belonged to a family of armoured dinosaurs called titanosaurs. The armour may have been used to support their weak backbones, or for defence.

Small, bony plates and spikes running along back

Dicraeosaurus means "double-forked lizard" because of the forked spines on its backbone. These may have helped to scare away predators. Some scientists believe that all diplodocids had spines but it is hard to know for sure because the spines do not often become fossilised.

DICRAEOSAURUS
(die-KRAY-oh-SAW-rus)

Family:	Diplodocidae
Size:	12 m (40 ft) long
Food:	Plants: treetop shoots
Period:	Late Jurassic
Range:	Africa: Tanzania

Apatosaurus was one of the dinosaurs discovered during the "Bone Wars" of the 1800s (see page 53). Its name means "headless reptile" because one of the first skeletons found did not have a head. It has also been called *Brontosaurus*.

APATOSAURUS
(a-PAT-oh-SAW-rus)

Family:	Diplodocidae
Size:	21 m (69 ft) long
Food:	Plants: treetop shoots
Period:	Late Jurassic
Range:	North America: Colorado, Oklahoma, Utah, Wyoming

Diplodocus had a tiny head at the end of a long neck, which stretched up to 7 m (23 ft) into the treetops. If attacked, it may have used its tail like a whip, lashing it at its predator with a force powerful enough to stun or even kill. Like other sauropods, it probably lived in herds.

DIPLODOCUS
(dip-LOD-oh-kus)

Family:	Diplodocidae
Size:	26 m (85 ft) long
Food:	Plants: treetop shoots
Period:	Late Jurassic
Range:	North America: Colorado, Montana, Utah, Wyoming

Neck as long as body

MAMENCHISAURUS
(ma-MENCH-ih-SAW-rus)

Family:	Diplodocidae
Size:	22m (72 ft) long
Food:	Plants: treetop shoots
Period:	Late Jurassic
Range:	North America: Utah, Colorado, Montana, Wyoming

Mamenchisaurus had the longest neck of all the diplodocid dinosaurs. Slender, bony supports grew out of each neck bone. These overlapped the bone behind, helping to support the neck's great weight.

Seismosaurus ("earth-shaking dinosaur") is maybe the longest animal that ever lived on land. Its bones were discovered in New Mexico, in 1986. Some are enormous: just one of its backbones is 1.5 m (5 ft) long. *Seismosaurus* probably weighed as much as 100 tonnes (98 tons).

SEISMOSAURUS
(SIZE-moh-SAW-rus)

Family:	Diplodocidae
Size:	38 m (125 ft) long
Food:	Plants: treetop shoots
Period:	Late Jurassic
Range:	North America: New Mexico

Stegosaurs

**The stegosaurs were large plant eaters
with triangular plates on their backs and
sometimes spikes on their tails and sides.**

Scutellosaurus
("lizard with little
shields") was an
ancestor of the stegosaurs and
ankylosaurs. Its back and sides
were covered with bony studs.

SCUTELLOSAURUS
(Skoot-EL-oh-SAW-rus)

Family:	Scelidosauridae
Size:	1.2 m (4 ft) long
Food:	Plants
Period:	Early Jurassic
Range:	North America: Arizona

KENTROSAURUS
(KEN-tro-SAW-rus)

Family:	Stegosauridae
Size:	5 m (16 ft) long
Food:	Plants: tough cycads
Period:	Early Jurassic
Range:	Africa: Tanzania

Kentrosaurus ("pointed reptile")
had a double row of plates and
spikes on its back and tail.
It also had spikes on its sides
for extra protection. If attacked,
it may have used its tail like a
weapon, swinging it from side
to side.

Long tail spikes

Weak teeth

Tuojiangosaurus was the first stegosaur to be discovered in China. It had a small, narrow head and a bulky body. Its teeth were small and weak, so it probably fed on young tender shoots and other soft vegetation.

TUOJIANGOSAURUS
(toh-HUANG-oh-SAW-rus)

Family:	Stegosauridae
Size:	7 m (23 ft) long
Food:	Plants: young shoots
Period:	Late Jurassic
Range:	Asia: China

Like those of other stegosaurs, *Stegosaurus's* plates may have been used to control its body temperature. In this case, they may have been covered with skin rich in blood vessels. If they were used as armour, they may have been covered with horn.

STEGOSAURUS
(STEG-oh-SAW-rus)

Family:	Stegosauridae
Size:	9 m (30 ft) long
Food:	Plants
Period:	Late Jurassic
Range:	North America: Colorado, Oklahoma, Utah, Wyoming

Small head

Horny beak

Armoured dinosaurs

There were two groups of armoured dinosaurs. The nodosaurs were covered with studs and spikes. The ankylosaurs also had tail clubs.

Boxlike head

Side spikes

Plates may have been covered with horn or with skin

SAUROPELTA
(SAW-roh-PEL-ta)

Family:	Nodosauridae
Size:	7.6 m (25 ft) long
Food:	Plants
Period:	Early Cretaceous
Range:	North America: Montana

Like other nodosaurs and ankylosaurs, *Sauropelta* ("shield lizard") could not run fast. Instead, if attacked it would crouch down on the ground to protect its soft underbelly, presenting its attacker with a mouthful of bony shields and spikes.

NODOSAURUS
(NODE-oh-SAW-rus)

Family:	Nodosauridae
Size:	6 m (20 ft) long
Food:	Plants
Period:	Late Cretaceous
Range:	North America: Kansas, Wyoming

Nodosaurus ("node reptile") had rows of small, bony knobs covering its back and tail, and oval-shaped plates on its back and hips. It had a narrow head and a heavy body.

Long shoulder spikes

PANOPLOSAURUS
(pan-OH-ploe-SAW-rus)

Family:	Nodosauridae
Size:	4.5 m (15 ft) long
Food:	Plants
Period:	Late Cretaceous
Range:	North America: Alberta, Montana, South Dakota, Texas

Panoplosaurus had broad, bony plates covering its shoulders and neck, and long spikes running down its sides. It had a larger head than most nodosaurs, with ridged teeth to grind tough vegetation.

Ankylosaurus was the largest ankylosaur. Its name means "stiff lizard" because its tail, made of fused bone, was held stiff and straight like the shaft of a club. At the tip of the tail was a lump of solid bone.

ANKYLOSAURUS
(ANK-ih-low-SAW-rus)

Family:	Ankylosauridae
Size:	11 m (36 ft) long
Food:	Plants
Period:	Late Cretaceous
Range:	North America: Alberta, Montana

Club tail could knock an attacker off its feet

SAICHANIA
(sy-kahn-ee-a)

Family:	Ankylosauridae
Size:	7 m (23 ft) long
Food:	Plants, especially semi-desert vegetation
Period:	Late Cretaceous
Range:	Asia: Mongolia

Bony spikes and plates

Saichania ("beautiful" in the Mongolian language) was a heavily armoured plant eater. Its head, like that of *Ankylosaurus,* was a box of armoured bone. Air passages in the skull lightened it and may have helped to keep the dinosaur cool by carrying moist air to its lungs.

Strong legs to support heavy body

Euoplocephalus ("well-protected head") is one of the best-known ankylosaurs. Bony armour fossilises easily, and many *Euoplocephalus* remains have been found in Canada.

EUOPLOCEPHALUS
(you-op-loh-KEF-ah-lus)

Family:	Ankylosauridae
Size:	5.5 m (18 ft) long
Food:	Plants
Period:	Late Cretaceous
Range:	North America: Alberta

TALARURUS
(tal-a-ROO-rus)

Family:	Ankylosauridae
Size:	5 m (16 ft) long
Food:	Plants, especially semi-desert vegetation
Period:	Late Cretaceous
Range:	Asia: Mongolia

Like other armoured dinosaurs, *Talarurus* had a horny beak, which it used to chop through tough vegetation. It also had cheek pouches to hold its food while eating.

Horned dinosaurs

The horned dinosaurs, or ceratopsians, were plant eaters that evolved during the late Cretaceous Period.

PSITTACOSAURUS

(si-TAK-oh-SAW-rus)

Family:	Psittacosauridae
Size:	2.5 m (8 ft) long
Food:	Plants, maybe fruit
Period:	Late Cretaceous
Range:	Asia: China, Mongolia, Siberia

Ridge holding strong jaw muscles

Horny beak

Psittacosaurus, or "parrot lizard", was named because it had a parrotlike beak and a square-shaped head caused by the ridge at the back of its skull.

LEPTOCERATOPS

(LEP-toe-SER-a-tops)

Family:	Protoceratopsidae
Size:	2 m (6½ ft) long
Food:	Plants
Period:	Late Cretaceous
Range:	Asia: Mongolia; North America: Alberta, Wyoming

Bony neck frill

Leptoceratops had the beginning of a bony frill at the back of its neck. In later ceratopsians, this evolved into huge neck frills.

Five-clawed fingers

97

CENTROSAURUS
(SEN-troh-SAW-rus)

Family:	Ceratopsidae
Size:	6 m (20 ft) long
Food:	Plants
Period:	Late Cretaceous
Range:	North America: Alberta, Montana

Centrosaurus ("sharp-pointed lizard") had a single horn growing from its nose, two smaller horns under its eyes and a neck frill with jagged edges. Like other ceratopsians, it relied on these to protect it from meat eaters.

Thick, pillarlike legs to support bulky body

PACHYRHINOSAURUS
(PAK-ee-RINE-oh-SAW-rus)

Family:	Ceratopsidae
Size:	5.5 m (18 ft) long
Food:	Plants
Period:	Late Cretaceous
Range:	North America: Alberta

Pachyrhinosaurus ("thick-nosed reptile") had a thick lump of bone on its nose rather than a horn, and a short frill at the back of its neck. It had a large, bulky body and weighed 3–4 tonnes (3–4 tons).

Styracosaurus was named
"spear point" because of the
long horn on its nose. It also
had several horns growing
from its neck frill.

*Horns used to scare
away or fight
predators*

STYRACOSAURUS
(sty-RAK-oh-SAW-rus)

Family:	Ceratopsidae
Size:	5 m (16 ft) long
Food:	Plants
Period:	Late Cretaceous
Range:	North America: Alberta, Montana

*Thick tail held out for
balance as it moved*

TRICERATOPS
(try-SERRA-tops)

Family:	Ceratopsidae
Size:	9 m (30 ft) long
Food:	Plants
Period:	Late Cretaceous
Range:	North America: Alberta, Colorado, Montana, Saskatchewan, South Dakota, Wyoming

Triceratops ("three-horned face") is
perhaps the best-known ceratopsian.
It lived in herds, like other ceratopsians, and probably
distinguished members of the same herd by the
number and arrangement of horns on their heads.

Boneheads and other plant eaters

Boneheads, fabrosaurs and pisanosaurs were plant eaters. They walked upright, on their hind legs, and probably lived in herds.

PISANOSAURUS
(pee-SAN-oh-SAW-rus)

Family:	Pisanosauridae
Size:	90 cm (3 ft) long
Food:	Plants
Period:	Late Triassic
Range:	South America: Argentina

Pisanosaurus was an early ornithopod. It was lightly built and looked like a large lizard. It ran around on its two back legs.

Lesothosaurus lived on the hot, dry plains of present-day Lesotho in southern Africa. It had sharp, pointed teeth shaped like small arrow heads, which it used to chew tough vegetation.

LESOTHOSAURUS
(less-OH-toe-SAW-rus)

Family:	Fabrosauridae
Size:	90 cm (3 ft) long
Food:	Plants
Period:	Early Jurassic
Range:	Southern Africa: Lesotho

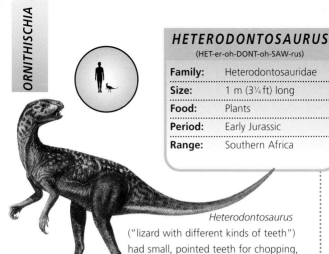

HETERODONTOSAURUS
(HET-er-oh-DONT-oh-SAW-rus)

Family:	Heterodontosauridae
Size:	1 m (3¼ ft) long
Food:	Plants
Period:	Early Jurassic
Range:	Southern Africa

Heterodontosaurus ("lizard with different kinds of teeth") had small, pointed teeth for chopping, larger back teeth for chewing, and two pairs of canine teeth for tearing its food.

STEGOCERAS
(steg-O-ser-as)

Family:	Pachycephalosauridae
Size:	2 m (6½ ft) long
Food:	Plants
Period:	Late Cretaceous
Range:	North America: Alberta

Like other pachycephalosaurs, *Stegoceras* (meaning "horny roof") had a thickened dome of bone on top of its skull. This bone was probably bigger in the males than the females and grew larger with age.

Five-fingered hands to grasp leaves and other vegetation

PRENOCEPHALE
(pren-oh-KEF-a-lee)

Family:	Pachycephalosauridae
Size:	2.5 m (8 ft) long
Food:	Plants, maybe fruit
Period:	Late Cretaceous
Range:	Asia: Mongolia

Like other boneheaded dinosaurs, *Prenocephale* walked on its two hind legs, holding its long tail out for balance as it moved. The tail would also have helped to balance the weight of its heavy head, which was surrounded with bony spikes.

HOMALOCEPHALE
(home-ah-loh-KEFF-ah-lee)

Family:	Homalocephalidae
Size:	3 m (10 ft) long
Food:	Plants
Period:	Late Cretaceous
Range:	Asia: Mongolia

Homalocephale belonged to a family of boneheads called the homalocephalids. Instead of having large domes on their heads, these dinosaurs had thickened skulls covered with bony knobs.

Pachycephalosaurus ("thick-headed reptile") was the largest bonehead and also had the largest dome on top of its skull, growing up to 25 cm (10 in) thick.

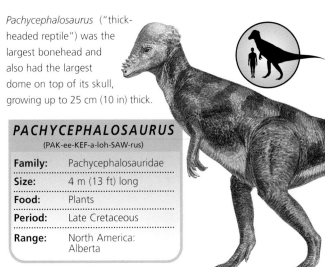

PACHYCEPHALOSAURUS
(PAK-ee-KEF-a-loh-SAW-rus)

Family:	Pachycephalosauridae
Size:	4 m (13 ft) long
Food:	Plants
Period:	Late Cretaceous
Range:	North America: Alberta

Although *Stygimoloch* ("horned devil") looked fierce and dangerous, it was really a peaceful plant eater like other boneheaded dinosaurs. The horns would help to frighten away any meat eaters.

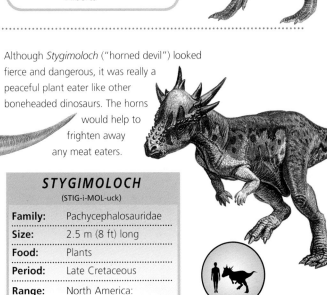

STYGIMOLOCH
(STIG-i-MOL-uck)

Family:	Pachycephalosauridae
Size:	2.5 m (8 ft) long
Food:	Plants
Period:	Late Cretaceous
Range:	North America: Montana, Wyoming

Hypsilophodonts

The hypsilophodonts were lightly built plant eaters. Like modern antelopes, they lived in herds and used their speed to escape from danger.

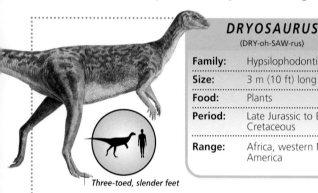

DRYOSAURUS
(DRY-oh-SAW-rus)

Family:	Hypsilophodontidae
Size:	3 m (10 ft) long
Food:	Plants
Period:	Late Jurassic to Early Cretaceous
Range:	Africa, western North America

Three-toed, slender feet

Dryosaurus was named "oak lizard", after its oak leaf-shaped teeth. It was one of the earliest, and largest, hypsilophodonts.

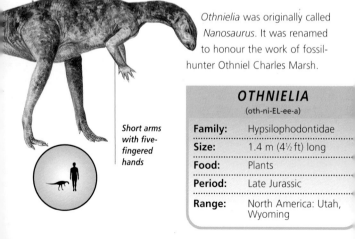

Othnielia was originally called *Nanosaurus*. It was renamed to honour the work of fossil-hunter Othniel Charles Marsh.

Short arms with five-fingered hands

OTHNIELIA
(oth-ni-EL-ee-a)

Family:	Hypsilophodontidae
Size:	1.4 m (4½ ft) long
Food:	Plants
Period:	Late Jurassic
Range:	North America: Utah, Wyoming

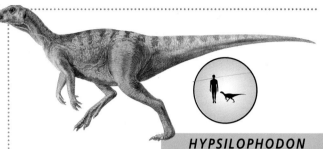

Hypsilophodon ("high ridged tooth") had no teeth at the front of its mouth. Instead, it had sharp teeth towards the back. It probably ripped off plants with its beak then chopped them up with its back teeth.

HYPSILOPHODON
(hip-see-LOAF-oh-don)

Family:	Hypsilophodontidae
Size:	1.5 m (5 ft) long
Food:	Plants
Period:	Early Cretaceous
Range:	Europe: England, Portugal

Thescelosaurus was larger than most of the other hypsilophodontids and may have been slower-moving. It had armour to protect it if attacked.

Rows of bony studs across back

THESCELOSAURUS
(thes-kel-oh-SAW-rus)

Family:	Hypsilophodontidae
Size:	3.5 m (11½ ft) long
Food:	Plants
Period:	Late Cretaceous
Range:	North America: Alberta, Montana, Saskatchewan, Wyoming

Iguanodonts

The iguanodonts were large, plant-eating dinosaurs related to the duckbilled dinosaurs. They evolved during the Jurassic Period.

Like other iguanodonts, *Iguanodon* ("iguana tooth") had spiky "thumbs" on its front legs, which it may have used to fight predators.

IGUANODON
(ig-WA-no-don)

Family:	Iguanodontidae
Size:	9 m (30 ft) long
Food:	Plants
Period:	Early Cretaceous
Range:	Europe: Belgium, England, Germany; North America: Utah; Africa: Tanzania; Asia: Mongolia

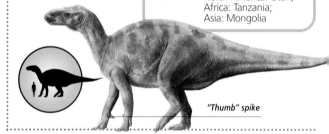

"Thumb" spike

OURANOSAURUS
(OO-ran-oh-SAW-rus)

Family:	Iguanodontidae
Size:	7 m (23 ft) long
Food:	Plants
Period:	Early Cretaceous
Range:	Africa: Niger

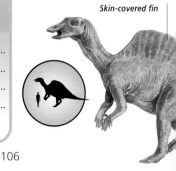

Skin-covered fin

MUTTABURRASAURUS
(MUT-a-BUR-a-SAW-rus)

Family:	Iguanodontidae
Size:	7.3 m (24 ft) long
Food:	Plants
Period:	Early Cretaceous
Range:	Australia: Queensland

Bony lump may have been used for display

Muttaburrasaurus, named after a place in Queensland where it was discovered, is one of the few dinosaurs known from Australia. It had a lump of bone on its long, broad head.

Like other iguanodonts, *Probactrosaurus* moved on all four legs but may have reared up on its hind legs to feed.

Hooflike nails on feet

Ouranosaurus ("brave reptile") had spines on its backbone, which may have supported a fin. The fin may have helped to control its body temperature by absorbing or losing heat.

PROBACTROSAURUS
(PROH-BAK-troh-SAW-rus)

Family:	Iguanodontidae
Size:	6 m (20 ft) long
Food:	Plants
Period:	Early Cretaceous
Range:	Asia: China

Duckbilled dinosaurs

The duckbilled dinosaurs, or hadrosaurs, had long, ducklike beaks. Some also had crests.

HADROSAURUS
(HAD-roh-SAW-rus)

Family:	Hadrosauridae
Size:	9 m (30 ft) long
Food:	Plants
Period:	Early Cretaceous
Range:	North America: Montana, New Jersey, New Mexico, South Dakota

Hadrosaurus ("big reptile") was the first dinosaur from North America to be named. Like other hadrosaurs, it had a long ducklike beak containing rows of flat teeth to grind up tough vegetation.

SHANTUNGOSAURUS
(shan-TUNG-oh-SAW-rus)

Family:	Hadrosauridae
Size:	13 m (43 ft) long
Food:	Plants
Period:	Late Cretaceous
Range:	Asia: China

Maiasaura, or "good mother dinosaur", was named after a complete *Maiasaura* nesting site found in Montana. Each nest was around 2 m (6½ ft) wide and spaced about 9 m (30 ft) – one dinosaur length – apart. This meant that each mother dinosaur could move around her own nest without disturbing the others.

MAIASAURA
(my-ah-SAW-rah)

Family:	Hadrosauridae
Size:	9 m (30 ft) long
Food:	Plants
Period:	Late Cretaceous
Range:	North America: Montana

Maiasaura *was too heavy to sit on her eggs but probably guarded them closely*

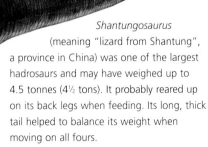

Shantungosaurus
(meaning "lizard from Shantung", a province in China) was one of the largest hadrosaurs and may have weighed up to 4.5 tonnes (4½ tons). It probably reared up on its back legs when feeding. Its long, thick tail helped to balance its weight when moving on all fours.

109

SAUROLOPHUS
(SORE-oh-LOAF-us)

Family:	Hadrosauridae
Size:	9 m (30 ft) long
Food:	Plants
Period:	Late Cretaceous
Range:	North America: Alberta, California; Asia: Mongolia

Saurolophus had a small, sloping crest that may have supported a flap of skin above its nose. By blowing air through this skin flap, *Saurolophus* could have made loud honking sounds to keep in touch with the rest of its herd.

LAMBEOSAURUS
(LAM-bee-oh-SAW-rus)

Family:	Hadrosauridae
Size:	9 m (30 ft) long
Food:	Plants
Period:	Late Cretaceous
Range:	North America: California, Montana, Saskatchewan

Lambeosaurus was named after Lawrence Lambe, a Canadian dinosaur hunter. It had a hollow, axe-shaped crest at the front of its head and a small, bony spike at the back.

110

CORYTHOSAURUS
(ko-RITH-oh-SAW-rus)

Family:	Hadrosauridae
Size:	9 m (30 ft) long
Food:	Plants
Period:	Late Cretaceous
Range:	North America: Alberta, Montana

Corythosaurus means "lizard with the Corinthian helmet" because its rounded crest looked like the headgear worn by Corinthian soliders of ancient Greece.

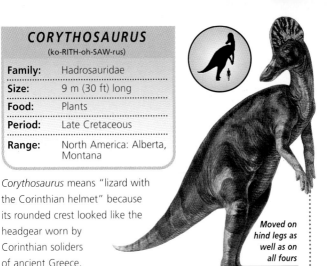

Moved on hind legs as well as on all fours

Parasaurolophus ("lizard with crest") had a thin, hollow crest nearly 2 m (6½ ft) long, which may have been used to make honking sounds. When it held up its head, the crest may have fitted into a small notch in its backbone.

PARASAUROLOPHUS
(par-a-SORE-oh-LOAF-us)

Family:	Hadrosauridae
Size:	9 m (30 ft) long
Food:	Plants
Period:	Late Cretaceous
Range:	North America: Alberta, New Mexico, Utah

111

Glossary

amphibians Animals with backbones and four legs that lay their eggs in water. The young pass through a larval stage before becoming adults. Modern amphibians include frogs and toads.

ankylosaurs Armoured dinosaurs covered with bony plates, knobs and spikes and with a bony club at the end of their tails.

beak A horny mouthpart on birds and some dinosaurs. Beaks are used in the same way as teeth, to hold and chop up food, but are lighter.

billion One thousand million.

boneheaded dinosaurs Dinosaurs with dome-shaped skulls of thickened bone to help to protect the males during head-on fights with other males. There were two groups of boneheads – homalocephalids and pachycephalosaurids.

camouflage A pattern or colour that allows an animal to blend in with its surroundings so that it cannot easily be seen by a predator.

carnivores Meat eaters.

ceratopsians Large plant-eating dinosaurs (also called horned dinosaurs) with pointed horns and big bony frills growing from the back of their skulls.

ceratosaurs Meat-eating dinosaurs that walked upright on their back legs and had small front legs. Some, such as *Ceratosaurus,* had one or more horns on their heads. Others, such as *Dilophosaurus,* had strangely shaped crests.

cheek pouches Small folds of skin at each side of an animal's mouth to hold food while chewing.

climate The usual weather in a place. Deserts have a hot, dry climate. Rainforests are warm and wet.

cold-blooded Used to describe an animal (such as a lizard or a snake) that cannot control its body temperature but must rely on the heat of the Sun to warm it.

continent A huge area of land on Earth. The continents are (from largest to smallest): Asia, Africa, North America, South America, Antarctica, Europe and Australia.

coprolites Fossilised dung, or droppings.

crest A bony structure on top of the head, usually used in display to warn away other males and win a mate.

Cretaceous Period Period of geological time from 140 to 65 million years ago. Dinosaurs were at their most varied during the Cretaceous Period but died out at its end.

cycads Non-flowering plants with thick trunks, no branches, and palmlike leaves; related to today's conifers.

digest To break down and absorb food into the body.

evolved Changed over many generations to produce a new body feature or a new species of animal.

extinction Death of every single one of a species. All the dinosaurs died out at the end of the Cretaceous Period 65 million years ago, along with animals belonging to other species.

family A group of related species of animal. For example, *Albertosaurus*, *Tyrannosaurus* and *Alioramus* are all part of the family Tyrannosauridae.

ferns Non-flowering plants with finely divided leaves called fronds.

fossils The remains of an animal or plant that have been preserved in rock.

gastroliths Stones found in the stomachs of some plant-eating dinosaurs to help them break down and digest tough vegetation.

ginkgoes Trees that look like conifers but shed their leaves in autumn. The only living species of ginkgo is the maidenhair tree.

habitat The surroundings in which an animal lives, including climate, water and plant life.

hadrosaurs Large plant-eating dinosaurs with long, flat beaks; also called duckbilled dinosaurs. Many hadrosaurs had crests on their heads. Hadrosaurs include *Parasaurolophus* and *Lambeosaurus*.

hatchlings Animals just hatched from eggs.

herbivores Plant eaters.

horsetail plants Plants with upright stems and tiny leaves; related to ferns.

hypsilophodonts Small, lightly built plant eaters that moved upright on their long, slender back legs.

ichthyosaurs Sleek, fast-swimming reptiles, similar in appearance to dolphins.

iguanodonts Medium- to large-sized plant eaters with hooflike nails on their hind feet and spikes on their hands instead of thumbs, which could be used to fight predators. The fifth finger on each hand could be bent across the palm to help an iguanodont grasp food.

Jurassic Period Period of geological time from 205 to 140 million years ago. Dinosaurs became common throughout the world during the Jurassic Period.

mammal-like reptiles Primitive reptiles with some mammal-like features (such as hair and teeth of different sizes) that lived before the dinosaurs; related to the ancestor of today's mammals.

mammals Animals with backbones and hair that give birth to live young and feed them on milk. Modern mammals include monkeys, whales, rabbits, cats and humans.

mass extinction A sudden dying out of many unrelated species of animal.

migration To move from place to place at certain times of the year in search of food or shelter, or to raise young.

minerals Substances that make up all rocks. Minerals are made up of mixtures of elements, such as aluminium, carbon, hydrogen, oxygen, potassium and silicon.

nodosaurs Armoured dinosaurs covered with bony plates, spikes and knobs.

order A group of related families. There are two orders of dinosaurs – Ornithischia and Saurischia. Orders are divided into smaller groups, called suborders. Suborders are divided still further into infraorders, divisions and families. For example, *Tyrannosaurus* belongs to the family Tyrannosauridae, infraorder Tetanurae, suborder Theropoda and order Saurischia.

ornithischian dinosaurs Bird-hipped dinosaurs. The Ornithischia order, or group, of dinosaurs includes horned dinosaurs, armoured dinosaurs, stegosaurs and two-footed plant eaters.

ornithomimids Fast-running, meat-eating dinosaurs with long necks and slender legs, similar in appearance to present-day ostriches.

ornithopods Two-footed plant eaters, including the iguanodonts, duckbills and hypsilophodonts.

palaeontologists Scientists who study palaeontology, the study of ancient (prehistoric) life from fossils.

phytosaurs Armoured reptiles that were the main meat-eating predators in rivers during the Triassic Period; similar in appearance to modern crocodiles.

plesiosaurs Swimming reptiles with paddlelike limbs that lived in the world's seas during the Jurassic and Cretaceous periods.

reptiles Cold-blooded animals with backbones, which lay eggs. Modern reptiles include snakes, crocodiles, lizards and turtles.

saurischian dinosaurs Lizard-hipped dinosaurs. The Saurischia order, or group, of dinosaurs includes all the meat-eating theropods and the plant-eating sauropods, or long-necked dinosaurs.

sauropods Long-necked plant eaters, such as *Diplodocus* and *Brachiosaurus*.

species A group of animals that look the same and breed with one another to produce young.

stegosaurs Large plant-eating dinosaurs with rows of triangular plates running down their backs and spikes on their tails.

tetanurans Large meat eaters, such as *Allosaurus* and *Giganotosaurus*. Tetanuran means "stiff tail" because the end of a tetanuran's tail was stiffened by interlocking bony structures. Tetanurans also had gaps in their jaw bones to help make their skulls lighter.

theropods Meat eaters, such as *Tyrannosaurus, Allosaurus* and *Struthiomimus*.

Triassic Period Period of geological time from 250 to 205 million years ago. The first dinosaurs evolved 230 million years ago, at the beginning of the Late Triassic.

vegetation Plant life.

warm-blooded Used to describe an animal (such as a mammal or a bird) that can control its body temperature.

Index

Note: Page numbers in *italic* refer to captions to illustrations. Main references are in **bold**.

International museums

Here are just a few museums with good collections of fossils. Exhibits may change as collections are added to, and dinosaur exhibitions may tour different museums.

AUSTRALIA
Queensland Museum, Brisbane, Queensland
Australian Museum, Sydney, New South Wales

CANADA
Redpath Museum, Quebec
Royal Ontario Museum, Toronto, Ontario
Tyrell Museum of Paleontology, Drumheller, Alberta

UNITED KINGDOM
Birmingham Museum, Birmingham, England
Natural History Museum London, England
Leicestershire Museum, Leicester, England
Museum of Isle of Wight Geology, Sandown, England
National Museum of Wales, Cardiff, Wales
Royal Scottish Museum, Edinburgh, Scotland
Sedgwick Museum, Cambridge University, Cambridge, England

UNITED STATES OF AMERICA
American Museum of Natural History, New York
Carnegie Museum of Natural History, Pittsburgh, Pennsylvania
Denver Museum of Natural History, Denver, Colorado
Los Angeles County Museum, Los Angeles, California
Peabody Museum of Natural History, New Haven, Connecticut
National Museum of Natural History, Washington, DC
University of Wyoming Geological Museum, Laramie, Wyoming
Utah Museum of Natural History, Salt Lake City, Utah

Web sites

Web sites are constantly being expanded or added. Check out:
www.tyrell.magtech.ab.ca/
Tyrell Museum homepage with fun pages and interactive programs.
www.cyberspacemuseum.com
(click on palaeontology) Database giving US museum information with access to other online palaeontology web sites.
www.austmus.gov.au
Australian Museum homepage.
www.nhm.ac.uk
Natural History Museum homepage.

Acknowledgements

l = left; r = right; b = bottom; t = top; c = centre

ILLUSTRATIONS
All art by **Steve Kirk**, except:
James Field (Simon Girling Associates), 25t, 43c; **Eugene Fleury**, 11t, 13t, 15t; **Mike Foster/Maltings Partnership**, 62–63b; **John Francis** (Bernard Thornton Artists), 59b; **Terry Gabbey** (Associated Freelance Artists), 54–55c; **Elizabeth Gray**, 28t, 33 tr & br; **Mark Iley**, 22, 41t; **Eric Robson**, 25b; **Martin Sanders**, 18–19; **Peter David Scott** (Wildlife Art Agency), 16, 17c & b, 23c, 24, 26, 29t, 30–31c, 32, 33b & cr, 39t & b, 43b; **Guy Smith/Mainline Design**, 8–9, 61t & c; 48–49c.

PHOTOGRAPHS
35 The Natural History Museum, London; 46t François Gohier/Ardea; 46b The Natural History Museum, London; 48 The Natural History Museum, London; 49t The Natural History Museum, London; 49bl François Gohier/Ardea; 49br The Natural History Museum, London; 50 Danny Lehman/Corbis; 51 Tom Bean/Corbis; 52t The Natural History Museum, London; 52b Ardea; 53tl Peabody Museum of Natural History, Yale University; 53tr The Natural History Museum, London; 53b Neg. No. 18502 Courtesy Dept. of Library Services American Museum of Natural History; 54 Jonathan Blair/Corbis; 55 Layne Kennedy/Corbis; 56 Michael S. Yamashita/Corbis; 57 François Gohier/Ardea.